Society of Homoeopathic Physicians of Iowa

Transactions of the Fourth Annual Session

of the Society of Homoeopathic Physicians of Iowa : held at Des Moines,

May 14th and 15th, 1873

Society of Homoeopathic Physicians of Iowa

Transactions of the Fourth Annual Session
of the Society of Homoeopathic Physicians of Iowa : held at Des Moines, May 14th and 15th, 1873

ISBN/EAN: 9783337869816

Printed in Europe, USA, Canada, Australia, Japan

Cover: Foto ©Andreas Hilbeck / pixelio.de

More available books at **www.hansebooks.com**

TRANSACTIONS

— OF THE —

FOURTH ANNUAL SESSION

— OF THE —

SOCIETY OF

Homœopathic Physicians

OF IOWA.

— HELD IN —

Des Moines, May 14th and 15th, 1873.

BURLINGTON, IOWA:

SNOW, FOOTE & Co., STEAM PRINTERS AND BINDERS, 115 NORTH THIRD STREET.

1873.

Society of Homœopathic Physicians.

OF IOWA.

OFFICERS FOR 1874.

PRESIDENT.
G. H. BLAIR, M. D.,.... ....FAIRFIELD.

FIRST VICE PRESIDENT.
A. O. HUNTER, M. D.,...DES MOINES.

SECOND VICE PRESIDENT.
DR. T. A. BENBOW,.......... ....NEW PROVIDENCE.

SECRETARY AND TREASURER.
G. H. PATCHEN, M. D.,..............................BURLINGTON.

BUREAUS AND COMMITTEES FOR 1874.

Board of Censors.
R. F. BAKER, M. D., Davenport;   S. P. YEOMANS, M. D., Clinton;
W. T. VIRGIN, M. D., Burlington;   P. H. WORLEY, M. D., Davenport;
P. W. POULSON, M. D., Council Bluffs.

Orator.
W. H. DICKINSON, M. D., Des Moines.

Alternate.
W. T. VIRGIN, M. D., Burlington.

Bureau of Materia Medica.
G. N. SEIDLITZ, M. D., Keokuk;   J. E. KING, M. D., Eldora;
W. T. VIRGIN, M. D., Burlington.

Bureau of Clinical Medicine.
L. E. B. HOLT, M. D., Marshalltown;   DR. T. A. BENBOW, New Providence;
A. O. HUNTER, M. D., Des Moines;   R. F. BAKER, M. D., Davenport.

Bureau of Obstetrics and Diseases of Women and Children.
S. B. OLNEY, M. D., Fort Dodge;   Mrs. R. H. HARRIS, M. D., Grinnell;
P. H. WORLEY, M. D., Davenport;   R. W. WATERMAN, M. D., Des Moines.

Bureau of Surgery.
W. H. DICKINSON, M. D., Des Moines;   E. A. GUILBERT, M. D., Dubuque.

Bureau of Medical Education.
C. H. COGSWELL, M. D., Clinton;   H. P. BUTTON, M. D., Iowa City;
E. JACKSON, M. D., Epworth.

Medical Electricity.
P. J. CONNELLY, M. D., Des Moines.

Bureau of Anatomy, Physiology and Hygiene.
A. O. HUNTER, M. D., Des Moines;   G. H. PATCHEN, M. D., Burlington;
P. W. POULSON, M. D., Council Bluffs.

Publishing Committee.
G. H. PATCHEN, M. D., Burlington;   W. H. DICKINSON, M. D., Des Moines;
R. F. BAKER, M. D., Davenport;   W. T. VIRGIN, M. D., Burlington;
E. A. GUILBERT, M. D., Dubuque.

Delegates to American Institute of Homœopathy.
W. H. DICKINSON, M. D., Des Moines;   P. H. WORLEY, M. D., Davenport;
G. H. PATCHEN, M. D., Burlington.

SOCIETY OF HOMŒOPHTHIC PHYSICIANS

OF IOWA.

Held in Des Moines, May 14th and 15th, 1873.

FIRST DAY—Morning Session.

The Society assembled at the Court House at 10.30 A. M., L. E. B. Holt, M. D., of Marshalltown, President, in the chair.

Dr. G. H. Patchen, of Burlington, was unanimously elected Secretary for the ensuing year, after which President Holt delivered an eloquent and practical opening address.

The Treasurer's report was read and passed into the hands of the Board of Censors for examination.

The following officers were elected for the ensuing year:

President—G. H. Blair, M. D., Fairfield.

First Vice President—A. O. Hunter, M. D., Des Moines.

Second Vice President—Dr. T. A. Benbow, New Providence.

The following physicians were elected to membership:

A. Wilson, M. D., of Ames; A. Kunze, M. D., of Davenport; R. W. Waterman, M. D., of Des Moines; Mrs. R. H. Harris, M. D., of Grinnell.

On motion, the paper of Dr. Blair, on Puerperal Convulsions, read before the Society last year, was ordered to be published in the proceedings of the present year.

The Society, on motion of Dr. Dickinson, went into committee of the whole on clinical experience.

Many interesting cases were related and discussed.

Dr. Hunter favored the Society with a very interesting case of puerperal convulsions with instrumental delivery. Gelseminum 1st, was the only remedy used; it controlled the spasms perfectly and carried the case to a happy recovery. A very peculiar feature was the disposition of the convulsions to return about a certain hour every afternoon, but the more frequent repetition of Gelseminum prevented the convulsions.

A case of extra uterine pregnancy was related by Dr. Dickinson. It had been diagnosed by a celebrated physician as a subperitoneal fibroid tumor of the uterus. A *post mortem* revealed a partial decomposed fœtus of about seven months, in the right fallopian tube.

Many other interesting cases were reported and discussed, after which the Society adjourned till 2 P. M.

Afternoon Session.

The Society met pursuant to adjournment, with an increased attendance.

The following amendment to Article VII of the Constitution was adopted:

" No physician who is not a graduate, and who has commenced the practice of Homœopathy since 1870, shall be admitted as a member of this Society."

The Committee on University question was continued another year, with a request to report after the meeting of the Board of Regents in June of the present year.

The Secretary read a notice of the death of Dr. W. C. Russell, of Calamus, in February, 1873, an esteemed member of the Society. After a few appropriate remarks concerning the life and character of the deceased, by Dr. Holt, a committee was appointed to draw up appropriate resolutions expressing the sentiments of the Society.

The resolution to meet annually in Des Moines was by a unanimous vote rescinded.

The next meeting, at the request of Dr. Blair, was decided to be held at Fairfield.

The following resolution, by Dr. Benbow, was adopted:

Resolved, That committees of different bureaus, and all persons giving their clinical experience, are requested to give the attenuation of the med icine used, and the frequency of the dose.

The Board of Censors reported favorably on the admission of Wm. Wilson, M. D., of Chariton.

BUREAU OF CLINICAL MEDICINE.

Dr. Benbow read a paper on Capsula Renalis reporting satisfactory progress, of a case of long standing and previous Allopathic treatment; was under treatment from February 16th to April 1st with remarkable improvement.

The Society listened to verbal reports upon epidemic Cerebro Spinal Meningitis. The experience of the different members showed that there is no specific treatment for the disease, but that a cold application—even pounded ice—to the base of the brain, and warm or hot baths to the body and extremities, produce the most favorable results, at the same time using Gelseminum, Belladonna, Bryonia, Veratrum Vir. internally, according to indications. Electricity—the positive pole to the cerival or dorsal region, the negative to the coccyx—has a very soothing and ameliorating effect, but is not a specific.

BUREAU OF OBSTETRICS.

Dr. Worley read an interesting case of amenorrhœa, which was ordered printed.

There was considerable discussion on the subject of ligation of the funis. Upon inquiry it was found that many physicians had been practicing non-ligation for the past two years, with no disastrous effects.

A case of congential Spina Bifida complicated with Scrotal Hernia, was reported by Dr. Holt. The Hernia was reduced and spinal trouble yielded entirely to the continued use of Nux Vom., in the 6th, 12th, 30th, and 200th attenuation successively.

The paper was placed in the hands of the publishing committee.

BUREAU OF SURGERY.

Dr. Blair, chairman, read an exceedingly interesting and instructive paper on syphilis—its history, course and treatment—containing some original and novel ideas.

Also a few reports of improved method of treating various surgical diseases, by Professor Danforth, of Hahneman Medical College, Chicago, which was received with thanks.

Dr. Dickinson reported the following cases:

1. Gunshot wound in the abdomen.
2. Removal of fatty tumor from inner angle of upper lid of right eye.
3. Removal of epitheleal cancer from lip.
4. Closing and healing of severe wound across the tongue, by wire sutures.

On motion adjourned till 8 o'clock P. M., to listen to the annual oration by S. P. Yeomans, of Clinton.

Evening Session.

At eight o'clock the Annual Oration was delivered before the Society by Dr. S. P. Yeomans, of Clinton. Owing to the ininclement weather the attendance was small. The oration was a masterly effort, evincing much ability and careful preparation. By resolution the thanks of the Society were tendered to Dr. Yeomans, and the paper passed into the hands of the publishing committee.

SECOND DAY—Morning Session.

President Holt in the chair.

The first thing in order was the report of Dr. E. A. Guilbert, chairman of the committee on securing the recognition of Homœopathy in the Medical Department of the State University.

To the President, Officers and Members of the Society of Homœopathic Physicians of Iowa:

GENTLEMEN—As professional engagements of a pressing character prevent my being present at your annual meeting, I forward, as Chairman of the Committee on Homœopathy in the State University, a brief report of progress. On the 26th of June last I received from Mr. Haddock, Secretary of the Board of Regents, a letter a copy of which I submit:

STATE UNIVERSITY, IOWA CITY, June 24, 1872.

E. A. Guilbert, Dubuque, Iowa:

DEAR SIR—On the 22d inst., on motion of Mr. Wilson, the communication of the Homœopathic physicians of Iowa was referred by the Board of Regents, to a committee of the Board consisting of Hon. C. W. Slagle, of Fairfield, and W. W. Merritt, of Red Oak, for consideration, who were requested to report to this Board at a subsequent meeting.

Very respectfully,

WM. J. HADDOCK, Sec'y.

I learn from two members of the Board of Regents that the Committee aforesaid will report at the forthcoming June session of the Board of Regents. Of course the nature of that report your Committee are unable to divine, but from the known views of several of the Board of Regents, we have reason to think that the said report will favor according us the recognition we ask, leaving the details as to the ways and means to be determined by further consideration. Speaking for myself, as I shall have no opportunity of ascertaining the views of the remainder of the Committee, I regard it as of great importance that the Society be represented at the June meeting of the Board of Regents. To that end I advise that the Committee be continued, and instructed to be present at Iowa City at the annual meeting of the Board of Regents of the State University. If this is done, I, for one, shall make every effort to be there, prepared to urge our claims to the best of my ability.

EDWARD A. GUILBERT,

Chairman Committee.

On motion the report was received, and the Committee instructed to confer with the Board of Regents at their meeting in Iowa City, in June, the expenses to be borne by the Society.

BUREAU OF HYDROPATHY.

An interesting case under this head was reported by Dr. Connelly, of Des Moines.

Dr. Benbow read some interesting cases, omitted under the proper bureau yesterday, which were placed in the hands of the publishing committe.

The retiring President, (Dr. Holt,) after a few remarks, thanking the Society for their earnest and efficient work and their harmonious and courteous bearing during the session, introduced the President elect, Dr. Blair, of Fairfield, to the dignity and responsibilities of his chair.

On motion the thanks of the Society were tendered Dr. Blair for his able efforts in behalf of the Society during the session; also to the press of the city and the State for so kindly noticing its proceedings.

The following Committees and Bureaus were then appointed:

BOARD OF CENSORS—R. F. Baker, Davenport; S. P. Yeomans, Clinton; P. W. Poulson, Council Bluffs; W. T. Virgin, Burlington; P H. Worley, Davenport.

ORATOR—W. H. Dickson, Des Moines.   *Alternate*—W. T. Virgin, Burlington.

BUREAU OF MATERIA MEDICA—G. N. Siedlitz, Keokuk; J. E. King, Eldora; W T. Virgin, Burlington.

BUREAU OF CLINICAL MEDICINE—L. E. B. Holt, Marshalltown; T. A. Benbow, New Providence; A. O. Hunter, Des Moines; R. F. Baker, Davenport.

BUREAU OF OBSTETRICS AND DISEASES OF WOMEN AND CHILDREN—S. B. Olney, Fort Dodge; Mrs. R. H. Harris, Grinnell; P. H. Worley, Davenport; R. W. Watermon, Des Moines.

BUREAU OF SURGERY—W. H. Dickinson, Des Moines; E. A. Guilbert, Dubuque.

BUREAU OF MEDICAL EDUCATION—C. H. Cogswell, Clinton; H. P. Button. Iowa City, E. Jackson, Epworth.

MEDICAL ELECTRICITY—P. J. Connelly, Des Moines.

BUREAU OF ANATOMY, PHYSIOLOGY AND HYGENE—A. O. Hunter, Des Moines; G. H. Patchen, Burlington; P. W. Poulson. Council Bluffs.

PUBLISHING COMMITTEE—G. H. Patchen, Burlington; W. H. Dickinson, Des Moines; W. T. Virgin, Burlington; R. F. Baker, Davenport; E. A. Guilbert, Dubuque.

DELEGATES TO AMERICAN INSTITUTE OF HOMŒOPATHY—W. H. Dickinson, Des Moines; P. H. Worley, Davenport; G. H. Patchen, Burlington.

On motion the Society adjourned to meet at Fairfield on the third Wednesday in May, 1874, at 10.30 A. M.

                              G. H. BLAIR, President.
     G. H. PATCHEN, Secretary.

OBITUARY.

WHEREAS, It has pleased the Master of Life to take from our midst by death our colleague and brother,

W. C. RUSSELL, of Calamus, Iowa.

Resolved, That this Society tender to the widow and son of the deceased our earnest and heartfelt sympathies in their bereavement, and that recognizing his worth as a man and a christian, his attainments as a physician and his merits as a citizen, we deeply feel his loss to the profession, to the church, and to society.

Resolved, That a copy of these resolutions be sent to the widow of Dr. Russell, and that they be spread upon the minutes of the Society.

W. H. DICKINSON,
G. H. BLAIR,   *Committee.*
P. H. WORLEY,

AN ADDRESS;

Delivered Before the Society of Homœopathic Physicians of Iowa,

By S. P. YEOMANS, M. D.

"KNOW THYSELF,"

Is an admonition that comes to us stamped with the impress of classical authority. Viewed from our stand point, its importance will be appreciated when we reflect that it implies an investigation of the wonderfully complex machinery that makes up the human organism, the dietetic and hygienic laws by which the vigor of health is maintained, and length of years secured; also of the agencies that tend to disturb normal conditions; and, last of all, of the curative means by which pain may be relieved. The vast field of enquiry which it requires us to explore has in all ages appalled the masses, and led them to be content to remain in ignorance, leaving to physicians the prerogative of working out these grand problems, deducing results, and enforcing obedience to their requirements by the dictum of scientific authority.' When we reflect upon the disgusting concoctions the sick have been compelled to take—the barbarous treatment to which they have been subjected and the results so far as the health and longevity of the race is concerned, we can but wonder at the patient endurance which has been exhibited, nor can we be surprised that from time to time the thoughtful and reflecting would venture to raise the earnest enquiry " Is this the best that science can do?" "Is there no balm in Gilead, no physician there?"—"Why then is not the health of the daughter of my people recovered?" It was this spirit that led the ancient Romans for six hundred years to prohibit the practice of medicine within their empire, and it is a sad commentary upon professional skill that the fact would never be known by the rate of mortality as recorded during this period.

Within the last century the same spirit has impelled many of the ablest members of the profession, as well as other gentlemen of culture, carefully to scrutinize medical theories, to put them to the test of close historical reading that results as shown by the ratio of mortality and advanced scientific research might be the measure of their value. It is the recorded verdict of those who have thus investigated, that the science of medicine has for two thousand years revolved around a common centre, never in a a single age advancing beyond its circumscribed orbit. While other departments of science and art, political economy, and industrial interests have indicated human progress and mental developement, it can scarcely be claimed that our profession is entitled to the credit of a single progressive movement since Esculapius delivered his oracular prescriptions, or Hippocrates bound his disciples by mystical oaths.

Careful observation has demonstrated that in acute diseases, recovery is the rule and death the exception, that these are self limited in duration and subject to natural laws, fixed and inexorable. In Typhoid Fever, for instance, only 16 per cent. will die with no treatment, and the average duration of the disease will be 14 days; while in Pneumonia 93 per cent will recover, the average illness being from 9 to 11 days. If medication can show no better results than this we had as well "throw physic to the dogs"— expend our money for something more useful and leave Dame Nature to deal with our ailments, unless we can bring to our aid the convenient theory, at one time quite generally entertained, that certain forms of disease are salubrious, as indicated by the old couplet—

> " An ague in the spring
> Is physic for a king."

If the authority of our own writers is to be credited the pathology of Fever, Inflamation, Pulmonary Consumption, and Rheumatism is no better understood, nor is the established treatment more successful than in the days of the Cæsars, Alexander or the Ptolemies. We can to day with no more certainty conjecture the force of the heart's contraction than could John Hunter. We are as profoundly ignorant of the functions of the Spleen and many other organs as was that prince of empirics, Paracelsus. Our ideas of the vis vitæ, of calorification, nutrition, or generation are not more clearly defined or philosophical than those entertained in the days of the Druids. Of the influence of catalytic forces in modifying chemical reaction, and changing the property of remedial agents the manipulations of the laboratory have thrown no light. Of the nature and properties of the specific poisons to which most diseases are supposed to owe their origin we have learned nothing of practical value from 3,000 years labor to discover some means of antidoting their destructive influences. Of the modus operandi of the drugs our patients are expected to take without question, we know no more than the rude and barbarous tribes of ancient times.

Addison, one of the profoundest thinkers and keenest observers of the age, says: "If we look into the profession of physic we shall find a most for- "midable body of men; a sight of them is enough to make a man serious, "for we may lay it down as a maxim that when a nation abounds in physi- "cians it grows thin of people. This body of men may be described like "the British army in Cæsar's time, 'some of them slay in chariots and "'some on foot.'"

Professor Oliver Wendall Holmes, of Boston, says: "If all the med- "icine in the world, except wine and opium, were thrown into the sea, it

" would be better for men and only worse for the fishes." He describes the practice of medicine as " the art of putting large doses of poisonous drugs " of which we know but little into living bodies of which we know less." Moliere, an eminent French physician, says: " Most people die of their " remedies and not of their diseases."

Dr. Adams, the learned translator of Hippocrates, says; " We cannot " think of the change in professional opinions since the days of John Hun- " ter without the most painful feelings of distrust in all modes of treatment."

In 1853 M. D' Feulins published in the Review Medicale, of Paris, sta- tistics of mortality of diseases in 1811 and 1851, from which it is shown that deaths from inflammatory affections had increased at least 54 per cent., from which he infers the decline of medicine during the preceding 40 years.

Dr. Forbes, who has been styled the modern Celsus, says: " In a large " proportion of the cases treated the disease is cured by nature and not by " the physician."

In Paris' Pharmacologia, esteemed for many years a reputable text book, we find the following on the subject of remedies: " It is impossible to cast " our eyes over such multiplied groups without being forcibly struck with " the palpable absurdity of some, the total want of activity in many, and the " uncertain and precarious reputation of all. Nor can we be surprised that " a portion of mankind has at once arraigned physic as a fallacious art, or " derided it as a composition of error and fraud."

Simon, a lecturer of wide repute on general pathology, says: " We do " not possess a complete medical knowledge of any single article of the " Pharmacopœia. It is a system of sham therapeutics—a blind empiricism " hostile to every interest of science and humanity."

Bichat, an eminent French teacher of medicine, says: " Materia medica " is no science at all for a methodical mind, but is a shapeless conglomer- " ation of inexact minds—of observations often puerile—of illusory reme- " edies—of formulas as oddly conceived as they are fastidiously arranged."

Magendie, who was excelled by no one in the profession, says in a lec- ture to a medical class: "Gentlemen, medicine is a great humbug. I " know it is called a science. Science indeed! It is nothing like science! " Doctors are mere empirics when they are not charlatans. We are as igno- " rant as men can be. Who knows anything in the world about medicine? " Gentlemen, you have done me the honor to come here to attend my lectures, " and I must tell you frankly in the beginning that I know nothing in the " world about medicine, and I don't know anybody that does know anything " about it. I repeat to you that there is no such thing as a medical science. " Who can tell me how to cure a headache?—or the gout?—or diseases of the " heart? Nobody! Oh! you tell me doctors cure people. I grant you peo- " ple are cured. Gentlemen, nature does a great deal; immagination does " a great deal; doctors do but little when they don't do harm."

The cause which above all others has served as a check to medical pro- gress may be expressed in the single word intolerance. No class of men, since the world began, have clung with more rigid tenacity to the maxims of the fathers than those of our profession. They have been clad with a mantle of charity broad enough to enable them to look complacently upon any impropriety that did not involve a departure from established precedents. This alone was the unpardonable sin for which no results, however salutary or beneficent, could atone. No argument so overwhelming or proof so conclusive as to outweigh the ingrained sentiment expressed by the Roman satirest:

> "Did Marcus say 'twas fact, then fact it is,
> No proof so solid as a word of his."

Neither fame, skill or learning could shield him who suggested an innovation or proposed an improvement, from proscription and an edict of excommunication as relentless, unyielding, and as formidable as was ever fulminated from the Roman Vatican for the suppression of heresy. No advance was ever made except through tribulation absolutely apalling, and success was never secured but by the common sense and discernment of the masses who dared to rebel against authority, however arrogant its assumptions. The guardians of the public health who should have been the most ardent advocates of reformatory movements have always closed their eyes to evidence, however palpable it may have been, like Gallileo's brother professor who stubbornly refused to look through the telescope lest he should see Jupiter's moons and thus be compelled to acknowledge his own theory fallacious.

In 1628 John Harvey first published the great fact of the circulation of the blood. Filled with apprehension of the terrible ordeal which he well knew awaited him, he withheld his discovery for eight years in order that he might fortify himself securely at all points against the charge of irregularity, and yet he was subjected to persecution the most vindictive, denounced in unmeasured terms as an imposter, and for a time so completely lost his popularity as to be almost without means of subsistence. After heroically breasting the storm of persecution for fourteen years, the French Academy, then the most learned body in the world, issued an authoritative edict declaring that the blood did not circulate through the body, and even thirty years later, in 1672, this astute body of infallibles reaffirmed their former decree, and added that Harvey's alleged discovery was an utter impossibility.

Before the time of Ambrose Pare hot irons, boiling oil and pitch were the only means used in arresting hemorrhage in surgical operations. This distinguished surgeon having, it is said, exhausted his supply of these materials upon a certain battle field, resorted, from necessity, to the ligature and simple dressings and to his unbounded surprise found that he had unwittingly made one of the greatest discoveries of the age. But the practice was so irregular and unscientific that the solons of the profession would not permit him to publish his discovery, and he was so persecuted for innovating upon regular medicine that he was compelled, for his own safety, to adduce garbled and incorrect statements from the old authors to prove that the discovery was made by them and not by him.

The discoverer of innoculation was persecuted with the most vindictive fury for fifty years. In 1774 the French Academy admitted its advantages after the princes of the royal blood, in opposition to their remonstrances, had been innoculated.

No discovery in medicine has been so fraught with blessings to the race as that of vaccination by Jenner. Previous to the adoption of this great prophylactic, one-tenth of the whole human family died from small pox. It is estimated to have prolonged the average duration of human life five years. In England alone there were 36,000 victims to this scourge in a single year, and yet for thirty years the war of the profession against Jenner was unprecedented. No terms of opprobrium were spared that could heap odium upon his head; nor were any means left untried that could tend to his humiliation and ruin. Even to this day fossilized specimens may be found who denounce the practice as quackery.

Peruvian bark was first discovered by the Indians of South America, and its introduction into popular practice, without having first received the sanction of the college, raised a storm of indignation against all who dared to use it. It is even recorded that the physician of Oliver Cromwell allowed him to die from ague rather than administer the hated specific. In 1609 the French Academy expelled one of its members for curing his patients with this interdicted drug. In the same year Besnir was expelled from the faculty of medicine for prescribing antimony.

Dr. Greenfield, a member of the Royal College of Physicians and Surgeons, was committed to Newgate on the complaint of the President of the College for daring to prescribe Cantharides. He published a vindication and the issue, says D'Quincy, ruined the unhappy doctor but taught his persecutors the safety and value of the practice.

Until comparatively a recent period the use of sulphur was not esteemed as regular. In 1640 Dr. Van Helmont contracted the itch and suffered many months rather than avail himself of this article. The titillation, however, finally proved too much for his dignity and led to his unconditional surrender to quackery.

The introduction of auscultation by the use of the stethoscope, and of percussion by which the condition of vital organs may be determined with almost absolute certainty, has met with the most bitter invective and violent opposition.

The production of anesthesia by chloroform, ether, &c., by which the severest operations are made painless, was denounced from Dan to Beersheba as an innovation so full of peril that no one having the least regard for human life would think of recommending it.

This blind subserviency to the antiquated dogmas of past generations has compelled the profession to retain formulas embracing the most absurd combinations which are condemned by the common-sense of the age in which we live. The "Theriaca Andromachi" was said to have been invented by Mithridates, King of Pontus, and was made up of seventy-two ingredients. According to Galen whoever took a proper quantity in the morning was insured from poison during the day; and according to the authority of Celsus, another father in Israel, Mithridates himself was so fortified against all baneful drugs that none would produce any effect when he attempted to destroy himself. Celsus tells us that it originally contained thirty-five simples, but that Andromachus, physician to Nero, added vipers and increased the number of ingredients to seventy-five. It is only within a few years that any one has dared propose to strike this compound from the British pharmacopia. Its rejection was moved by the late Dr. Heberden, and upon a division it was found that thirteen members of the college voted to retain it while fourteen favored its rejection. The orthodoxy of the French has been more inflexible, as this preparation is still retained as officinal in the Codex Medicamentaris of Paris. The latter standard authority also still retains the absurd formula of Deist for the preparation of an extract of Opium, which directs the decoction to be boiled incessantly for six months.

Now before we award to the ancients the prerogative of dictating medical law to all coming ages, it is seemly proper to enquire who the fathers were, and what were their claims to so exalted a privilege?

Esculapius outranks all others of whom we have reliable historical knowledge, and is styled par excellence the father of medicine. He was of Grecian birth and ranked among the gods. It was believed that he was removed from earth at the request of Pluto who complained that he performed so many cures as to rapidly diminish the number who died. His cures were wrought in temples, the disciples or priests being bound by a solemn oath to confine the mysteries of the science to a single family. Upon the application of patients for treatment an animal was first offered to the gods, then the prophetic tripod was mounted and the oracular prescription communicated. These healing temples were multiplied throughout Greece, and at one time there were 100 in the Roman Empire. We know but little of the treatment, but it is presumed to have been orthodox as we are informed that Aristides, the Greek, was ordered by one of these oracles to lose 120 pounds of blood. The unhappy man not having so much in his own body wisely took the liberty of interpreting the prescription in his own way and parted with no more than he could spare.

Hippocrates claimed to be the seventeenth lineal descendant of Esculapius. He taught that there were but two fluids in the body—but one word to express nerve, ligament, and tendon; but one for an artery, vein or excretory duct; that the cause of disease was to be sought in meteorological and astronomical changes. The main articles of his materia medica were Hellebore, Colocynth, Elaterium, Copper, Onions, Garlic, Parsley, Wine, Honey, and Cantharides. His authority was unquestioned for ages.

Asclepiades, a Greek physician born B. C. 91 years, ranks among the most distinguished of the medical patriarchs. His arts, says Pliny, were such as every fashionable physician employs—soothing the patient and avoiding everything that can give pain till nature cures him or he sinks under the disease. He taught that the principal cure of a fever was the disease itself; that many diseases could be cured by the sound of the flute,

3

He recommended the trumpet for the cure of Sciatica. We are told by Zimmerman that this practice prevails in Chili; that the physicians blow around the beds of their patients to drive away disease. He says they think their knowledge is complete when they are skilful blowers. Medicine men among the Indians retain the same method in the practice of their art. We need not go to heathendom to find doctors well skilled in this direction.

Celsus is awarded a position among the most eminent old-time professional worthies. Of his remedies that have come down to us by regular succession are the warm blood of a recently slain gladiator—a certain portion of human flesh, with many others equally disgusting.

Of all the medical law makers of antiquity none were more distinguished, had a wider or more enduring fame than Galen. Of the many works attributed to his fertile brain, eighty-three are esteemed genuine. He taught that there were four distinct humors—blood, phlegm, yellow and black bile—and three distinct kinds of auras, gases or spirits—natural, vital and animal. A modern author of acknowledged repute says: "The "hypothesis of Galen, respecting the virtues and operation of medicines is "a web of philosophical fiction which was never surpassed in absurdity." Dr. Paily calls it the preposterous system that for more than thirteen centuries gave universal laws in medicine to Europe, Africa and part of Asia. Dr. Cullen says his theory is false and inapplicable.

Paracelsus was unquestionably a charlatan, and yet his claims to eminence cannot well be denied, as he was regular and strictly orthodox. He was the first professor of chemistry, and introduced the use of mercury—ever since esteemed the very Sampson of Allopathic remedies in all ages and countries. He adopted the wildest theories of the alchemists, and ostentatiously claimed to have discovered the long sought elixir that would cure all diseases and give immortal life and health, He was compelled to flee from place to place to avoid the vengeance of his dupes, and finally died a drunken vagabond with a bottle of his Catholicon in his pocket.

These are but a few of the most prominent great professional lights to whom we trace our antiquity, and at whose shrines we are to worship with all the ardor of Eastern devotion, under the pains and penalties of excommunication as medical heretics and infidels.

We claim to have found a better curative system than that of our fathers, and we have chosen to rebel against authority however ancient or imposing may be its demands. Voluntarily assuming the consequences of our temerity we appeal to the common sense and sober reason of mankind for the value of the sentiments we maintain. Our well known motto, "*Similia Similibus Curantur*," expresses the chief peculiarity of our system. We claim that drugs which in the healthy person produce morbid conditions will in diminished doses remove like conditions when they present themselves in disease.

This is not a proposition based upon any preconceived theory, nor is its verity dependent upon any analogical process of reasoning. It is one the truth or falsity of which is susceptible of demonstrative proof by the simplest and most conclusive tests so easy of application as to be within reach of any honest enquirer after truth.

It would serve no good purpose to attempt to explain how or why this result is attained. It is one of those mysterious and inexplicable phenomena with which we are so often confronted when we attempt to investigate the laws of our being. We are content to know the fact, though we may not be able to explain the rationale of the process. We may, however, very properly take our bearings and see how far we have departed from the orthodox faith and whether after all there may not be some question as to our heresy.

Dr. Jones says: "Mercury causes congestion of the liver, and jaundice, "and in small doses it will cure the same diseases."

Cazenaw, in his work on the skin, says: "Eczema is often produced by "mercury, and it may be cured by the same drug in small doses."

Pereira, in his Materia Medica, says: "Arsenic will both cause and "cure convulsions, fevers, and diseases of the skin." The same fact is repeated in Christison and Griffith's dispensatory.

Twedie says: "Belladonna produces an eruption similar to that of "scarlatina," and Dr. Gardner says "it is an incomparable remedy in this "disease."

Dr. Dixon says the most marked case of ague he ever saw was caused by Quinine. It is needless to say that this remedy is esteemed a specific for ague. He also says that silver causes shivering and fainting sensations, and that it will remove like symptoms when due to other causes.

Dr. Richardson says, "Kreosote will cause or cure vomiting according to "the dose."

Dr. Earlinger says: "It is well known that an obstinate diarrhœa is "among the remote effects of Opium, and yet this is the chief remedy for "the cure of this affection."

Leppelletier says: "Tartar emetic will produce dyspepsia and engorge. "ment of the lungs if given in health, and will in small doses remove these "conditions and induce resolution in this disease."

These are not the views of merely exceptional men in the profession but are facts of universal recognition. Neither is the acknowledgment of the homœopathic law limited to the remedial action of the articles mentioned. None will presume to question that Alum, Muriate of Ammonia, Rhubarb and many other drugs will purge in large doses and constipate the bowels in small; that Ipecac will vomit or arrest vomiting according to the dose given; that Gentian and Nux Vomica in large doses debilitate the stomach and impair digestion, while in small doses they act as a tonic in dyspeptic subjects; that Sanguinaria, Quinine, and Opium may be stimulant or sedative according as we graduate the dose.

The most severe paroxysms of congestive fever can scarce be distinguished from the poisonous effects of Opium, and yet the very highest Allopathic authorities pronounce this the most reliable remedy. Prof. Bell advocates its use in the strongest manner. "What," says he, "it will be exclaimed by "some, Give Opium, a narcotic, in a state of apparent apoplexy or stupor "which may be said to resemble narcotism?"

These examples, familiar to the practitioners of every school, will suffice to show how the regulars, with all their boasted reverence for the teachings of the fathers, have been inadvertantly compelled, by the logic of events, to gravitate towards our law of cure, or rather, if you choose so to regard it, how small the angle of the line of divergance that has led us away from the ancient faith. To these concessions which with our allopathic friends are mere incidents having no significance with reference to any general principles, we supplement our own experiments made with a view to determine the fact whether they are not indices pointing to a law establishing the relation between all other drug symptoms in the healthy, and curative remedies in disease. It is not too much to say that the men who have prosecuted this investigation were fully qualified for the task assumed, nor that they were animated by a desire to reach the truth. No test could be less liable to the charge of unfairness. It was conducted in strict accordance with the inductive system of the Baconian school of philosophy. Deductions were left to the development of facts and not predicated upon preconceived theories. Most of the leading remedies of the old school and many others of whose virtues we had no knowledge, were taken in variable doses by persons in full health and all the symptoms produced, carefully noted from day to day, and hour by hour. The reports of these collected and collated constitute our materia medica and become valuable as evidences only as by treating the sick it is found that symptoms and morbid conditions respond to the remedies which are proven to produce corresponding results in health. Every case of disease that has come under our management has afforded us an additional opportunity to test the great principle upon which we believe the law of drug action depends. While we may admit that we have not always succeeded to our entire satisfaction, we affirm that our failures have arisen from an inability always to determine with absolute certainty the remedy that most nearly covers the totality of the symptoms and not from a want of adaptability of our therapeutical law to any given case that may occur. We claim that the experience of three-fourths of a century has been a most triumphant vindication of the views of Hahnemann. That under the most violent opposition, and in the face ·of proscription and intolerance, we have compelled an honorable recognition, and extorted from an incredulous public the confession that we merit a full share of confidence as members of the healing art.

Our infinitesimal doses have subjected us to the most unmeasured ridicule. We might dispose of this point summarily by the averment that our system does not, nor never has assumed to fix the homœpathic dose. It has always been esteemed the prerogative of the practitioner to select such potency as his own experience determined to be most effective. Nevertheless we are free to admit that we do not measure the value of medicine by the quantity given. Neither do we deny that we claim that our most satisfactory results are frequently attained by medicine carried to a degree of attenuation that some might deem extravagant. It is safe to assume that it is quite as difficult for the allopathists to explain upon any rational theory how massive doses operate to remove disease, or how it is that they are able now to carry supplies in the vest pocket which twenty-five years since required a huge pair of saddle-bags as it is for us to make clear the modus operandi of our prescriptions. We submit that if the researches of twenty-five centuries have not enabled them to comprehend the rationale of drug action according to their method of appreciation that we ought surely to be allowed a single century for investigation and to be exempt from the charge of ignorance even though we may not be able to give a lucid reason for all the facts we may witness. In reflecting upon the immediate causes of disease no one can avoid the conclusion that morbific agents exert their influence in a condition of the most extreme tenuity. A healthy, vigorous man journeys through a malarious region and is attacked with an intermittent fever that may cling to him for months. Another may, for a few days, inhale the atmosphere of the tropics and become the victim of yellow fever. One may receive a letter from a friend a thousand miles distant, and while reading its contents be infected with the small pox contagion that in some mysterious way has clung to the paper. The obstetrician may go from a patient suffering from puerperal fever, may thoroughly fumigate his person and apparel, and ten or twenty days hence communicate the disease to another patient. The farmer may visit his market town while the cholera is prevailing there, spend an hour, return home in good health and fall a victim to the disease in less than twenty-four hours. The physician may visit a case of Scarlatina, travel a hundred miles in his round of visits and then by simply pausing to shake the hand of some favored child communicate the seeds of disease or death. In all these examples, and hundreds of others might be adduced, there is a specific material cause so infinitesimally minute that the chemist, though he may detect the thousandth part of a grain of Arsenic, Iodine, or Strychnine, cannot with all his reagents, discover a trace of it. A scale, though so nicely graduated as to determine the weight of the smallest fraction of matter, cannot weigh it. Neither can a glass though its magnifying power may bring to view an atom inconceivably small determine its existence, and yet possessing a virulence sufficient to permeate every fibre of the system, to disturb the functions of every organ, the action and relation of every cell and molecule—to send the seething blood through its vessels—to produce the most intense agony, reducing the strong to the helplessness of infancy, the most intellectual to imbecility, and leading multiplied thousands to untimely graves. If, in the full vigor of health, with the conservative powers of nature the *vis medicatrix naturæ* in full force, causes so minute, so apparently insignificant thus impress the human organism, what does reason and common sense teach us to expect when impossibility is intensified by disease?

In health we may without inconvenience direct the eye to a light of great intensity, but let inflammation attack this sensitive organ and a single ray will produce the most unsufferable agony. Darken the room, bandage the eye, produce Egyptian darkness and yet the obscuration of the sun by an intervening cloud will be readily discerned. The burly Teuton may tax his gastric powers with half a gallon of lager beer and a pound of cheese without realizing that he has a stomach, but let acute inflammation seize this organ and a teaspoonfull of the blandest fluid will be instantly rejected. In inflammation of the brain the softest notes and sweetest music may produce convulsions.

If the result of disease is thus to increase sensibility to all external impressions, is it not absurd and preposterous to expect to calm the storm and restore the excited organs to their normal condition by massive doses that in robust health must of necessity produce the most serious derangement of the animal economy? Is it not an attempt to extinguish fire by casting on additional fuel? Does it not commend itself to one who will give the subject a moment's reflection as at variance with every principle of reason, science or philosophy?

Let us turn our attention once more to our allopathic friends and see if we cannot glean something from their voluminous annals that will fortify us in our convictions of the efficacy of minute doses. In 1847 Dr. Hunt published a volume on the treatment of skin diseases. On page 14 of this work he says: "One quarter of a drop of Fowler's solution, three times a "day, has in a few weeks effected a permanent cure of an exceedingly "troublesome disease." The British and Foreign Review accepts the case as genuine and remarks that each dose contains only the 480th of a grain of Arsenic. They tell us that the active principle of Ipecacuanha is emetine which constitutes only 14 to 16 per cent. of the crude drug, and one-twelfth and even one-sixteenth of a grain of the latter is conceded to be strictly an orthodox dose. This would equal about one-hundredth of a grain of emetine. There are but few practitioners who have not witnessed examples of dyspepsia, hemorrhage and other symptoms of the most alarming character resulting from simply removing the cork from a bottle of Ipecac in a close room.

In Paine's Institutes of Medicine we are told that in certain conditions here is nothing comparable with Calomel in doses of one-sixteenth to one-twentieth of a grain once in 4 to 12 hours. It is well known that crude Mercury has no medicinal effect, yet mixed with simple conserve of roses and thoroughly triturated so as to divide and break up the globules precisely as we treat our remedies, the result is Blue Mass, a compound of the highest rank in allopathic esteem. In 1810 two vessels received on board several tons of crude Mercury saved from the wreck of a ship near Cadiz. In three weeks the whole crew of 200 men were mercurialized; two died, and all the animals, including a canary bird, rats, mice, even cockroaches were destroyed. Here was an article wholly inert and insoluble, yet capable of exhaling a vapor which when attenuated by mixture with atmospheric moisture became a virulent poison.

Dr. Paine says: "I have seen in my own family the most formidable "cases of remittent fever, when hope of recovery had been abandoned, "yield to less than a single grain of Quinine divided into sixteen doses."

Dr. Trumbull says one-hundredth part of a grain of Aconite made into an ointment and applied to the skin has produced a sensation of heat, pricking and numbness which continued a whole day.

Pereira and Sigmond tell us that a dilatation of the pupils may be pro_ duced by only approximating the leaves of Hyosciamus or Belladonna to the eyes.

Paine says violent erysipelatous inflammation over the whole surface of the body is often induced by approaching within a few yards of a certain species of Rhus.

Paris in his Pharmacologia says the matter of febrile contagion is in creased in activity by moisture of the atmosphere. Plague is most common in Egypt after the inundation of the Nile, and he seems to have caught a glimpse of the true principle of attenuation, as he adds: "I am well sat- "isfied that the regulation of a dose of medicine is more important than it "is generally supposed to be. Substances perfectly inert and useless in one "dose may prove in another active and valuable. Medicinal substances," he adds, "are more readily absorbed in small than large doses," and that "extreme pulverization assists the operation of all substances whose active "principles are not easily soluble."

Dr. Murray says: "Unpleasant symptoms have been experienced by "merely keeping Aconite for some time in the hand."

The Lobelia Longiflora spreads such deleterious exhalations around it that asthmatic oppression of the chest is felt on approaching within many feet of it. Darwin thus alludes to it:

> "And fell Lobelia's suffocating breath,
> Loads the dark pinions of the gale with death."

Dr. Routh, in a tract designed to oppose Homœopathy, frankly admits that small doses, especially in large dilution, will often times act very sat isfactorily. He says: "I have seen this repeatedly."

It is believed that the efficacy of Cod Liver Oil, so extensively used in pulmonary disease, is largely due to the 40,000th part of Iodine which it con- tains. The various Mineral Springs of the world which enjoy so wide a reputation as health restorers owe their virtues to various saline compounds so largely diluted and so minute in quantity as to require the most skilful chemical analysis to detect their presence.

Mr. Liston, certainly the peer of the most eminent surgeons of Europe, after a fair trial of our leading remedies under the direction of a Homœo- pathist, has had the candor to express in a published letter his entire satis- faction with the results obtained. He even expresses the regret that the power of Aconite was not known to him earlier, as he was convinced that it would have prolonged the life of his father whose death had been hastened, in his opinion, by ill-judged copious venesection.

With these statements, which are only a sample of an unlimited supply at command from the same source, we are content to rest our case, leaving our allopathic friends to the full enjoyment of all the merriment they can derive from our Liliputian doses.

Theorize and speculate as we may with regard to scientific abstractions we shall fail thus to satisfy the practical demands of an enquiring public. There is an argument in results as indicated by facts and figures, that will outweigh all the learned theories that science can present. To the sick the dogmas of antiquity and the disputations of doctors sink into insignificance in comparison with the absorbing question, What are my chances for recovery?

In most of the larger cities of Europe and America, we have had for several years, in active operation public hospitals and dispensaries. These are mostly established by authority, and are under the surveillance of inspectors who carefully note results and make official reports of the same. These reports have the same claims to public confidence as those which emanate from Allopathic institutions of like character, and by comparison therewith the respective merits of the two systems of practice may be fairly judged. Few cities in the world have more perfect hospital regulations than Vienna. Both systems of practice are recognized by law, and each is granted the same privileges and subjected to the same requirements. From their official published reports we find the rate of mortality as follows: From Pleurisy, in Allopathic Hospitals, 13 per cent.; in Homœopathic Hospitals 3 per cent. From Peritonitis, 13 per cent. in Allopathic and 4 per cent. in Homœopathic Hospitals. From Dysentery, the former lost 22 per cent. and the latter 3 per cent. From Fever, the Allopathic mortality was 6 per cent. against 2 per cent. under our treatment. Without entering into details, we may present as aggregate results in the hospitals of London, Edinburgh, Glasgow, Liverpool, Vienna, and Leipsic, as given upon the authority of Dr. Routh, an Allopathic Physician, as follows:

In Allopathic Hospitals, mortality.................... ....10 5 per cent.
In Homœopathic Hospitals, mortality....................... 4.4 per cent.

In New York City during a period of five years the rate of hospital mortality as shown by authentic reports was under Allopathic treatment 14.36 per cent. while under Homœopathic treatment it was only a fraction over 7 per cent. The Cholera statistics of Vienna in 1836 show the rate of mortality under Homœopathic treatment to have been 33 per cent., against 66 per cent. under Allopathic. In the same disease in Edinburgh, in 1849, our school lost only 25 per cent. while the mortality under other treatment was 66 per cent. Cholera reports from Liverpool and all other places are equally favorable to our system.

In St. Margarite's hospital of Paris, 100 beds were appropriated to a physician of our school. An attempt was made, by petition, to induce the authorities to annul the privilege thus granted, which they declined to do and stated as a reason therefor that during the years 1849 1850-1851, as shown by legal evidence before them, the rate of mortality under Homœopathic treatment was 3 per cent. less than under any other system of practice. These are matters of public record having the verity of official documents. They may be known, read and scrutinized by all men. To them we invite attention, and challenge investigation, and are willing to abide the verdict that common intelligence may award.

And now, as we again meet at our annual convocation and survey the field we have abundant reason to rejoice and take fresh courage for the conflict which must continue during the period of our labors. We have achieved vastly more than could have been expected during the few years of our history. Our numbers, influence and patronage have multipled at a rate which may well astonish our foes as well as ourselves. We are not only honored by an occasional nod of recognition by the dignified worshipers of antiquity, but we have absolutely compelled them to so modify their therapeutical ideas as to promise speedily to vie with us in the minute ness of their doses. We have almost banished from existence that relic of barbarism, the lancet. The world may well say of the profession as Robert Emmett, the great Irish orator, said to the judges who condemned him: "If all the innocent blood which you have shed was collected in one vast "pool your lordships might swim in it." But let us be thankful that we may truthfully appropriate the language of Macbeth to the ghost of the murdered Banquo:

> "Shake not your gory locks at me,
> Thou can'st not say I did it,"

In all important reformations success and progress are mainly dependant upon incessant toil and arduous labor. We have yet much to learn. Every case submitted to our care and skill becomes a subject for profound study. The ever varying shades of symptoms that disease presents will, if carefully studied, lead to investigations and results that will continually add to our knowledge and usefulness and tend to the success of our principles.

There is still another qualification that is imperatively required if we would acquit ourselves as true reformers and worthy members of the medical profession. I remember hearing Prof. Ludlam say to his class that in a certain condition of impending Puerperal Convulsions by simply catching the eye of your patient and holding it by a steady gaze you may safely tide her over the most imminent peril; but, he added, a condition precedent to the exercise of this mental or psychological power is a moral status upon the part of the practitioner that will command the confidence and esteem of the pure and virtuous.

It may well be questioned whether this moral fitness is not quite as essential to the successful treatment of other forms of disease. The readiest converts and the most ardent friends of our system are found in the higher

4

stratum of society, among the intelligent, cultivated, refined and virtuous, and it is well to remember that the laws of chemical affinity are not more fixed than those of social affinity. To gain position and hold a place in these higher circles we must merit it by possessing the qualities which entitle us to claim it. If we are gross, vulgar, intemperate or licentious, we must expect to sink to a level with that class whose habits and vices are congenial to our tastes, and it is well to be prepared for the failure which must inevitably result. If on the other hand we are true to the teachings of pure morality and the principles of our school we shall succeed, and instead of the long predicted period when our Allopathic friends shall hold a joyful *post mortem* over our remains we shall witness them as with elongated faces they will fall into a funeral procession and with mournful cadence join in the refrain—

> " Pity the sorrows of a poor old man,
> Whose trembling limbs have borne him to your door—
> Whose days are dwindled to the shortest span—
> Oh, give relief, and heaven will bless your store."

BUREAU OF SURGERY.

G. H. BLAIR, M. D., Fairfield, Chairman.

—

SYPHILIS, by GEO. H. BLAIR, M. D.

Periodic literature, the text books of our schools, and even special treatises upon the subject are, unfortunately, deficient, not only in the proper considerations of the distinctive diagnostic signs of Syphilis, but, if one may judge from following the treatment prescribed, they lack also in the means recommended for its medical and surgical conduct.

Of the causes of these unfortunate errors and omissions it were perhaps idle to speak. The want of practical experience of many writers, and hence their *secundem artem* statements and precepts; the fear of unpopularity in urging a treatment at variance with the views of the high-potency advocates—those gentlemen who profess such a holy horror for the knife and the cautery and who shudder at the mention of a palpable drug—and the general disinclination to handle so foul a theme, have each probably had their influence in producing this result. But there is no one grand division of disease—in this instance incorrectly so-called—thus ranking it with Psora and Scrofula, and frequently confounding it with each, which merits, in a higher degree, our closest investigation.

In justification of the production of this paper, permit me to remark, that my experience in the treatment of this disease has been quite extensive. The control of a Seaman's Hospital, wherein it is safe to say that nine-tenths of those who were admitted either were suffering, or had at some previous period been afflicted with Syphilis; and years of management of the Protestant Orphan Asylums of Columbus and Cleveland, in which, for the most part, the unfortunate little inmates were picked up from that class of community who would in all probability transmit to their offspring any hereditary taint, together with a large private practice connected with this disease, (a thing we are not apt to boast of!) leads me to assume that I am at least deserving of a hearing, and that the conclusions arrived at are worthy your careful consideration.

One more preliminary digression, which seems not inappropriate just here. For a quarter of a century I have been a believer in, and practiced strictly in accordance with the law of *Similia*. While using both the very low and the extreme high potencies as the exigencies of the case may seem to require, I recognize no man's right to dictate any limited degree of strength of their administration. A knowledge of the Materia Medica, with a clear appreciation of the importance of observing aggravations in disease, will enable one to disregard, in a great measure, the various hypotheses and theories advanced by either extreme of combative dilutionists. Farther on I offer a suggestion which may afford you something of a clue to the selection of potencies—a suggestion occurring from the often-observed-efficacy arising from its adoption and application.

Just a word more and I will enter upon the subject. Perhaps this paper might properly have been limited to the *treatment* of Syphilis alone; but I have thought proper to enlarge its scope sufficient to briefly, but it is hoped intelligibly, characterize some of the more important forms of Syphilis; to express some well considered opinions regarding its infection and transmissibility; to notice some of its complications, and demonstrate the vast superiority of our remedial agencies over those of the Old School.

Of the history of Syphilis we have very imperfect and uncertain information of its early prevalence, nor are we acquainted with the precise nature of its inception and formation. There are those who see traces of the disease in Scriptural references. Avicenna and Valesca describe a disease probably identical with it as prevailing during the latter part of the 14th century; many date its origin coeval and connected with the discovery of America, &c., &c. Since the time of Columbus, we have been able to trace its course in modified forms with some degree of clearness—sometimes raging as a virulent contagion, the breath of, or even contact with, those affected, being sufficient for its production. You will remember that one of the counts in the indictments against Cardinal Wolsey, was that he infected the King of France by means of his breath alone. In the early Franco-Italian wars, in the war of the Crusades and in the intercourse of the Spaniards with the Sandwich Islanders may be seen instances of its infectious poisoning.

The nature of the original disease has, however, become changed and modified, or rather certain phases of the original poison have set up an independent condition of a pathological nature capable of propagating itself. This latter observation is one of much moment and should be carefully considered, for whereas *true* Syphilis is a disease of the gravest character, its off-shoots are comparatively harmless and easily amenable to treatment. A mistake in the diagnosis may be productive of the most serious consequences. This assertion, involving the question of the hereditary nature of the affection will be briefly alluded to hereafter.

The time for the development of chancre—the first invariable evidence of pox—varies greatly; it has been detected as early as the second day after *coitus*, and on the other hand, has been delayed apparently for months. Usually, however, we may look for its appearance between the fifth and tenth days, no premonitory symptoms presenting prior to its development. A slight itching is at first experienced, followed, or accompanied, by small pimples filled with matter. These soon assume the form of an ulcer, possessing peculiar appearances and characteristics, according to the nature of the poison; a fact to be speedily determined would we feel easy respecting the treatment to be pursued. The most important diagnostic signs for the determination of true Hunterian chancre are: its appearance, as a rule singly, rarely more than one appearing, although two, or even three may exist in exceptional cases; the surface of the sore is regular and disposed to be circular; the centre assumes a grayish tint; the edges slope inwardly; the bottom has a smooth, lardaceous appearance; the formation of pus is slow and quantity scant; and more important than all, *there is a hard, rigid, circumscribed base* and the edges of the ulcer may often be observed to be indurated also.

Fortunately, this form of Syphilis is comparatively rare, probably not comprising more than one-sixth of the whole number of cases occurring. This, likely, is due to the slight secretion from the ulcer; but from whatever cause, certain it is, the virulence of its contagion is much less than that of chancroid.

Now, this is the chancre to be quickly detected and speedily removed by the surgeon, especially since the absence of pain and irritation and the tardiness of its formation, unluckily too often prevent its discovery until the constitutional taint becomes inevitable.

The *simple chancre, or chancroid,* possesses well defined characteristics, which, if uncomplicated, render its detection quite easy. Its edges are perpendicular and serrated; the floor of the ulcer is uneven and honey-combed, as it were, with a grayish exudation therefrom profuse in quantity; the areola of the ulcer is, besides being much less regularly circumscribed, darker in color, and the edges and the base instead of being hard and indurated have a peculiar elastic feeling on pressure, the nature of which can only be understood by those who are experienced. Simple chancre generally appears in groups, seldom singly, and is accompanied with much pain and tenderness.

It is not deemed necessary to sub divide these ulcers into the various forms adopted by writers who enter minutely into the consideration of this subject. The two varieties just described constitute, in fact, the source of all others; and hence the phagedenic, the sloughing, and, indeed, all the other described sores of venereal origin are but modifications or complications with other vitiated conditions arising from the two forms. Indeed, to be precisely correct, we may attribute the remote source of *all* forms of Syphilitic ulcer to *tru chancre* alone, since the distinctions are of comparatively recent date.

Ricord has stated that, for the first five or six days of its existence, chancre may be always considered a strictly *local affection,* and the opinion is undoubtedly correct. Hence, local treatment should be resorted to, with a certainty, if promptly and energetically applied, that no secondary results will follow. Were we absolutely certain of the nature of the primary sore we might possibly leave it to take care of itself, if a simple one; but since it frequently is complicated in its nature, and occasionally might deceive the most skillful diagnostician, it were best to use an indiscriminate treatment in all forms of chancre. For this purpose, in the case of an individual of largely scrofulous or strumous diathesis, one in whom the lymphatics are easily agitated and irritated, the use of the knife is earnestly advised— complete extirpation of the ulcer, including the additional surrounding tissue to a breadth at least equal to the diameter of the surface of the ulcer, unless there should exist an abnormal hemorrhagic tendency, when cauterization should be preferred. In the ordinary forms of ulcer the remedies to be employed for their removal are—relatively to their importance— *Nitric Acid, Nitrate of Silver, Paste of Sulph. Acid and Charcoal, and Caustic Potash,* always bearing in mind the importance of a thorough and deep application, one sufficient to penetrate to the sub-cellular mucous tissue, which is the base of the chancre. The highly lauded *Vienna Paste* has proved in my hands very unsatisfactory, for the reason that, forming a crust over the top of the ulcer does not allow a knowledge of the extent to which it has penetrated; and if we wait for its removal and successive applications, too much time is lost for purposes of safety. One thing, however, must especially be borne in mind: *That no energetic treatment for the speedy destruction of the ulcer should be resorted to after well-defined induration is present,* as this is a certain indication that the disease has already become constitutional.

The lesson to be impressed is this: Whether the sore be either chancre or chancroid, its quick removal may prevent secondary results, and in any event can prove of no disadvantage. Those who through ignorance, for it can be called nothing else, oppose local treatment, not only protract the disease, but endanger the health and the lives of their patients.

After the reproductive process commences, evidenced by granulations, exudation of healthy un-inoculable pus, simple dressings of lint, saturated with pure water are sufficient, unless, indeed, the progress should seem somewhat indolent, when a weak solution of some stimulating application, as the Sulphates of Copper or Zinc, may be used with advantage.

As before remarked, the primary indication or early stage of chancre, needs but a local treatment, but lest a possible mistake in diagnosis may occur, an anticipatory or preventive means may be properly encouraged, inasmuch as under no circumstances can any bad result follow under our system of medication. A low regimen, frequent bathing, entire freedom from sexual excitement and the administration of the proper remedies, should not be neglected. In individuals of scrofulous diatheses *Hepar. Sulph., Cal. Carb., Silicia, or Sepia* may be given; but in the majority of cases the different preparations of *Merc.,* particularly the *Iodide* and *Biniodide* will prove of most value. More will be said of the different phases of ulcer when we come to treat of remedies and the indications for their use.

' We come now to consider the more serious aspects of this often-times frightful disease as manifest in its *second* or constitutional stage. If not controlled in its first or inceptive period within the limited time suggested— say five or six days—the poison becomes absorbed by the lymphatics—not by the veins as formerly supposed—and is first evidenced by the formation of *Bubo*. This manifestation may proceed from either the true or the simple chancre; indeed may result from gonorrhœa or other irritating causes; but when appearing in connection with, or following a primary sore, their nature is, of course, easily determined. In men, the inguinal gland, if from inoculation of the *Penis*, is the ordinary seat of bubo. In women, as frequently, it may be found situated between the labiæ and the thighs, or round ligaments. But wherever manifesting themselves or whatever the point of inoculation, the treatment should be the same—always taking into consideration, however, the character of the virus from which they spring. Considering then, that the bubo arising from *simple chancre* or *chancroid*, as our modern writers term it, is the termination and ultimatum of the disease, it were better perhaps, if possible, to disperse it before suppuration takes place, inasmuch as no further ill consequences will ensue. For this purpose pencillings with *Iodine Tinct.* or the application of *Iodine ointment*, together with the administration of the same remedy internally, in dilution, will ordinarily suffice, provided always that its application is *early*. If, however, the abcess progresses to an extent where fluctuation may be distinctly felt, our object should be to promote suppuration as speedily as possible, until the point of safely using the lancet is reached. *Silicia, Hep. Sulph.*, or *Apis.* claim a consideration here, together with the use of warm emollient poultices. But if the progress of the bubo be particularly slow, with much swelling, involving the surrounding parts, it will be advisable to give outlet to the deep seated and scanty pus, by means of *Caustic Potash*. Particularly if there be reason to suspect ramifications into cellular and sub-cellular tissue, will this prove the most available, as well as most satisfactory means of evacuation. *Pressure*, under these circumstances, by means of adhesive straps, is also an advisable auxiliary in expediting a cure.

In my estimation it is neither desirable nor proper to attempt the suppression of bubo where a consecutive of the *true* chancre. On the contrary, every endeavor should be made to hasten its consummation, that the virus may have in part a means of escape, without expending its full force throughout the general circulation. The means to be employed are identical with those employed for promoting suppuration in the other form of bubo; but whereas in chancroid abscess a speedy effort should be made to heal the wound, if languid and indolent, we should on the other hand probably favor the long discharge of pus in the bubo arising from true chancre. In this connection it may be mentioned that the pus of either variety of bubo is inoculable, each transmitting its own peculiar virus, and hence care should be exercised in its contact.

Space in a paper of this character will not allow of a more extended allusion to chancre and bubo. To the treatment recommended exceptions will, no doubt, be taken by some ultra practitioners who denounce *local* treatment for *anything;* and also by those deluded beings who regard chancre as but the external manifestation of a constitutional taint; but the actual practical observation of a few hundred of these cases will, I apprehend, soon modify their opinions. Besides, no man should be conceeded the right to criticise whose experience in the treatment of the disease under consideration has been closely limited.

We come now to the consideration of the graver stage of the affection, wherein the general constitution has become poisoned, and technically termed *Lues Venerea*. Most authors have divided this into a *Secondary* and *Tertiary* stage—the latter of which should more properly be called the *Mercurial* stage, inasmuch as I undertake to say that nearly every symptom connected with it, is either the direct result of mercurial poisoning alone, or its complication with, or aggravation of the original disease. Out of the multitude of cases passing under my immediate observation, I have yet to see one unconnected with a system thoroughly saturated with Mercury, even affected with periosteal inflammation which might not have arisen from other than a Syphilitic cause; nor under an enlightened Homœopathic treatment exclusively, have I met with a single instance of nodes, caries, or necrosis.

Usually, secondary symptoms develope themselves in from three to six weeks, although there are both earlier and later exceptions. As a general rule, no manifestations of an unusual character, except the light febrile disturbance which frequently attends all abscesses, as well as bubo, are the precursors of its existence. In my own experience the throat has given the earliest indication of the general taint, though perhaps the skin is as often the index. The throat, tonsils and fauces take on but little of the soreness and inflammation which commonly precede the formation of an ulcer—indeed the full development of ulcer being sometimes the first observable sign of any affection of the parts. Generally, however, the tonsils assume a pale or dark appearance; there is a slight exudation of mucous over the surface, the center of which grows rapidly darker, and terminates in an ulceration, the secretion from which is of a peculiarly *sticky* character. In some instances of a virulent nature, sloughing takes place and even gangrene, occasionally, though rarely, may follow; but this seldom results unless complicated with scrofula, struma, and more often with Mercury. Following the throat affection or coincident with it, eruptions of the skin make their appearance, and in so many and diverse forms as to almost defy description without means of ocular demonstration. However, for the sake of partial completeness, some of the more prominent manifestations will be mentioned, leaving a more diversified description to be embraced in the symptoms which call for the appropriately selected drug remedies.

Ordinarily the skin, especially in the neighborhood of the penis and vulva; between the thighs and nates; under the arm-pits, and in other protected parts becomes affected with small mucous papules. They are of a copper caste, slightly elevated and usually granulated. Over the general surface of the body, but more particularly the chest and forehead, they assume the appearance of small, hard lumps, exuding a secretion which dries quickly, is easily rubbed off, and is again reformed. They are generally circular in form, small in size, and as a rule, terminate without serious painful annoyance, although they occasionally ulcerate, and sometimes degenerate even to sloughing. They are known under the name of *mucous tubercles*.

In the milder forms of constitutional taint, roseola pemphigus, herpes and the lesser manifestations of exanthema and erythema develope themselves, and nothing but a knowledge of the history of the case would lead to a suspicion of their venereal origin. In fact it is questionable whether they be the direct or indirect results of syphilitic virus.

Of the various forms of lichen, lepra, psoriasis and even of vesicular eruptions, it were impossible to speak at length in this article.

Aside from the actual knowledge of the early history of the case, perhaps the most prominent indication for a suspicion of the true nature of the disease is the almost universal presence of the *copper color* attending. Even Hahnemann attached so much importance to this peculiar coloring, that he regarded its disappearance as a diagnostic sign of a speedy, if not already radical cure. Allopecia, induration of the testicles and pulmonary Syphilis are conditions of so questionable a nature as being the direct result of specific virus, as not to merit present consideration. As before remarked, the so-called *tertiary stage*, being the effect of Mercurial abuse, will also be ignored in the examination of Syphilis proper; but the complications evolved will be considered when we make our selection of remedies.

The question of the hereditary transmissibility of Syphilis is a debatable one, as is also the extent of its contagion or infection. Time was, perhaps—indeed the fact is indisputable—when the disease was terribly infectious; but it has become so modified and lessened in its virulence and so much more readily yields to treatment, that we need not apprehend a return to this manner of its propagation. Instances have occurred under my own observation, which to the superficial observer would seem to have been developed without innoculation; but a thorough history of the patient has invariably revealed the fact that it was simply a latent virus reproducing the old manifestations of a previous period, or that innoculation had taken place in some unusual manner.

Of its hereditary nature I am inclined to be exceedingly skeptical. That dyscrasias of various kinds and indeed any ill-conditioned and impoverished condition of the system is apt to impress fœtal life and hence be noticeable in the child, is certain; but that a genuine Syphilis with its undoubted and undeniable characteristics is transmitted from mother to child I unhesitatingly deny. The mere fact that exanthemata, pemphigus, and other suspicious skin eruptions and even nodes are found in the infant without previous chancre, amounts to nothing. They may each be the product of scrofula, and some of them may even be diseases of fœtal life. There is much more reason to suspect that the inoculation of the child by the mother during labor is the secret of any well marked case of Syphilis in the child. A strong point favoring this assertion is the fact, well attested by most of those conversant with the subject, that pox if not developed in the infant within the first six months of existence, may not be expected thereafter to develope itself. Of the asserted instances of nurses having been contaminated from suckling children in whom Syphilis was trans-

5

mitted, they should be regarded with great distrust. Neither the blood, the milk, the semen, nor in fact any natural secretion of the body is inoculable. Physicians of large experience in venereal disease know only too well the beastly proclivities of men, aye, and even women, of low degree, when under the influence of wine and sexual passion, to always attribute the appearance of a primal chancre in the mouth or upon the mammary glands to the lips of the innocent infant.

It is unfortunate that the great reverence entertained for the founder of our school, should have led so many of his disciples to adopt his errors in common with his truths. The idea of chancre being but the external man. ifestation of a constitutional taint, is so easily demonstrable of fallacy that it seems really preposterous. Indeed it is perfectly safe to guarantee abso. lute immunity from constitutional affection, provided we can be thoroughly satisfied that it receives our attention within four or five days of the appearance of the primary sore. But, unfortunately the chancre is sometimes concealed in the urethra and within the folds of the vagina, and being thus unrecognizable is absorbed before a suspicion of its existence is entertained. Hence, from this cause alone, has probably arisen the theory of blood contamination before the appearance of chancre.

Directly at variance with the doctrine that Syphilis is hereditary, and, paradoxical as it may seem, authors who sustain this view, at the same time contend that by prophylactic means it can be speedily and thoroughly exterminated, thus rendering our mode of treatment a subject to be placed among the "Lost Arts." And this observation, giving rise to reflection upon the means to promote so desirable an end naturally suggests the propriety of licensing houses of prostitution, or rather permitting their establishment under proper restrictions—for licensing implies payment, and no community should attempt to benefit itself by, or even receive the "wages of sin." I approach this subject tenderly, lest offence be given to the namby-pamby sentimentalism which so eminently characterizes the age. But certain it is, that so long as human beings remain as at present constituted, just so long will unlawful sexual commerce prevail. No moral suasion, no legal enactments can prevent it. Dating at least from the time of King David, we have had continuous evidence of the truth of this assertion. How then to prevent the physical evils arising therefrom becomes a question of great importance, and one to which the medical philanthropist should turn his attention. *If*, (a little word we are too often compelled to use,) if our judges, our law-makers, our constabulary, and to bring up the rear, our *doctors*, were wise, honest and efficient; if a thorough supervision, a thorough examination, and a thorough enforcement of sanitary measures, could be accomplished there are strong reasons for permitting the establishment of these houses under strict requirements, at least until venereal disease became obliterated—"a consummation devoutly to be wished." But this is, in some sort, another digression, so I pass on to my subject proper.

How long does it take to cure *Lues Venerea?* This question is one often anxiously asked, and its answer depends up the form which the disease assumes, which tissues are involved, and especially whether it be present alone, or whether it be complicated with scrofula or mercurial poisoning. Ordinarily it is as amenable to treatment as any of the diseases of a chronic nature. In referring to the records of the U. S. Marine Hospital, at Cleveland, O., while under my charge, I find that the average number of days treatment was 50. For the treatment of the primary sore 64 days were sufficient—and this includes time of convalescence, or in other words the period from the entrance to the exit of the patient. In private practice, owing to the fact of not having so complete control of the patient, I admit my success has hardly equalled this result, although from the data now at my command, the time employed has not averaged more than twenty additional days. Included in this estimate are several cases in which the Syphilitic affection had been complicated with other diseases. Under favorable circumstances, and without mercurial combinations—or, what amounts to the same thing, *when the patient has not been handled by an Old School doctor,*—we may anticipate still more favorable results. Contrast with this the assertion of Ricord, in one of his more recent letters: That he would not even undertake the cure of a case of *lues venerea* unless the patient would pledge himself *to remain at least one year under mercurial treatment!*

Each succeeding year, apparently, lessens its malignant type, but whether this be due to its disappearing *ex mero mortu*, or is owing to a more enlightened treatment is a matter of speculation. Were I a believer in its hereditary transmission, I should account for it upon the principle of *safety from inoculation*, since a large proportion of this world's people would now have Syphilitic poison, in a greater or less degree, coursing through their veins. But, from whatever cause, certain it is that even within my own time the disease has become essentially modified and more yielding to treatment.

I do not recognize *Sycosis* as having any necessary connection with either Syphilis or Gonorrhœa, much less, as being a combination of the two, as generally taught. It were much better, in a scientific point of view to discard this idea altogether, and to consider that fig-warts, cauliflower excrescences and other various fungi included under this name, are the results of an entirely independent poison. They are often observed without the presence or previous existence of chancre or chancroid, and even gonorrhœa, although the latter is a frequent accompaniment. The most important proof of the correctness of the view I have advanced is that they do not yield to the ordinary treatment for Syphilis and gonorrhœa; and contrary to the course to be pursued in the two latter, viz: *the administration of the low potencies,* we must to be promptly successful here, administer the higher dilutions. Sycosis is really a state of hyperæmia—Syphilis, a state of waste and exhaustion. And herein lies the hint in relation to the selection of potencies, to which I have before alluded, a hint which long observation and experience has convinced me should be given. *In cases of blood poisoning characterized by rapid degeneration, loss of tissue, cachexia and anæmia the low potencies should be preferred; on the contrary if there should be hyperæmia, morbid growths, fungi, condylomata, &c., without waste, select the high potencies.*

Fig-w.i   s in the male, when situated upon the *glans penis* or upon the prepuce   metimes attain to such a size as to produce phimosis or paraphimosis, and therefore if the surgeon has reason to suspect such a result he should at once clip them off with the scissors.

Cauliflower excrescences, especially in the female, also sometimes reach to great size. I have in two or three instances observed the vagina so completely filled with them that it was with difficulty that an injection could be thoroughly applied. Such a condition giving rise to the retention of the secretions is apt to engender ulceration and sloughing, and hence excision should also be resorted to here.

Allow me two or three observations which have been omitted in their proper places, and the *general treatment* of Syphilis will be considered. I note the without system or order, as the few days intervening since I commenced the preparation of this article have been seriously disturbed by my professional calls.

Sycosis poisons the general system with or without the appearance of bubo. No local treatment alone will prevent a farther development *Syphilis*, too, if we are to credit the testimony of most authors, makes its secondary onslaught oftener without, than with bubo. This *may* be so, but *I have yet to see a case in which* the constitutional disease became developed in which *there was not, at least, perceptible glandular irritation, if not well-developed bubo.* That little brain called *ganglia, must* swell with indignation at the approach of the virus.

Of the reported cases of syphilitic poisoning from vaccination, that is, from the use of the scab taken from individuals laboring under syphilitic dyscrasia, they should be received with caution. Of course the presence of the disease being known, no physician would willingly use vaccine from such a source; hence if we accept the theory that Syphilis is promulgated in this manner, we must also believe that the vaccine virus was obtained from the child to whom the disease was transmitted, or, from one in whom there was no suspicious external manifestations—in short that the blood of such persons is inoculable. At Camp Chase, in 1862, I observed seven or eight individuals undoubtedly poisoned with Syphilis by vaccination. Having peculiar views concerning this subject I was induced to investigate the matter closely. It may be imagined it was exceedingly difficult to get at the truth, but the result was finally accomplished. It appeared that the whole company to which these men belonged had been vaccinated at the same time with the same virus. Those who were poisoned were the *first ones to submit to the operation*, the remaining sixty or seventy being subjected only to the mild symptoms which ordinarily follow. The inquiry revealed the fact that *the physician had used the same lancet with which, in the morning, he had opened a true Syphilitic bubo,* and hence the cause was easily accounted for, a result which might have otherwise staggered my non-belief in the hereditary doctrine. Again, the same year, I developed in the family of a scrofulous friend of mine, with the use of genuine *cow pox virus,* eruptions, which, in the absence of absolute knowledge, would at once have been pronounced Syphilitic. I may add that the matter was introduced with the blade of a new pocket-knife, which had never before been used for a similar purpose, and that the virus, applied in several other cases was productive of the most beautiful results. Thus you see how easily one may be led astray in forming an opinion, unless he give the closest examination in detail. I may add, that the only way to dispel any doubt as to the nature of the case, is by inoculation.

In common with all writers and experimentalists, I rank the different, preparations of *Mercury* foremost in the treatment of true, uncomplicated Syphilis. To one acquainted with their provings this statement may seem superfluous, since it is a matter of difficulty, often times, to the inexperienced, to distinguish between Mercurial and Syphilitic poisoning. There are, however, indications and conditions which point to the use of one or the other of the different preparations, and to these I call your attention.

In true Syphilis, then, when it runs a natural course, or when there is reason to believe no complication exists, *Merc. Solubilis* should be preferred. I am well aware of the fact that Hahnemann in his later days discarded this preparation—the child of his own begetting— or, at least, gave preference to *Merc. Vivus*. Perhaps my early prejudice in favor of the former preparation was due to a remark made me by the venerable Prof. Pulte, many years since, to the effect that no apprehension of any ill-result might be entertained in its use, *however low the potency*, inasmuch as he had frequently given it in such doses as to produce laxation of the bowels, if not catharsis, without any appreciably bad result. This may naturally be inferred as the result of the combination of Mercury with Nitric Acid, which probably, in some manner antidotes its tendency to develope a poison, *sui generis*. I believe, with Teste—discarding his ridiculous notion that the sex of the individual should determine the selection—that so far as the important indications calling for their use is concerned, *Merc. Vir.* and *Merc. Sol.* may be used indiscriminately ; with this consideration in favor of the latter,: that whereas we should always prescribe it in the 1st, 2d, or 3d trituration, and its use is frequently to be of long continuance, we can guard against a possible bad contingency.

When the disease seems to predominate in the glandular system as evidenced by swelling, induration and abscess, I give preference to *Iodide* and *Bin Iodide* of Mercury, particularly the latter. If there be rapid disorganization and sloughing of the affected part, *Merc. Corrosicus* may be given. Cinnabar and the red precipitate of Mercury have been highly extolled by many, especially by our German cousins, but I confess I have never had occasion for their use. In alluding to the use of these varieties as above, you will of course understand that the corresponding symptoms, indicating the employment of Mercury, are implied. Briefly, Mercury may be given with success in almost any case of true, unadulterated Syphilis, as well as in many of its complications. It is particularly valuable where mucous surfaces are involved, especially in inflammation and ulceration of the throat and mouth, in pustular and tubercular eruptions, and in those cases where from combination with some latent dyscrasia, especially scrofula, nodes and affections of the osseous system generally, have been developed. It may with propriety be given from the appearance of the chancre (as a means of prophylaxis) throughout the successive stages of the disease. Do not take it for granted, however, as have most of our Homœopathic writers, that because of the disappearance of the primary sore, the medicine affected the removal. *Post hoc, sed ne propter hoc*, should be substituted for *post hoc, ergo propter hoc*, since the truth is, nearly nine-tenths of these sores being not truly and purely syphilitic, will disappear of their own accord. It is amusing to note the owl-like gravity with which so many of our authors, such as Lutze, Laurie, Attomyr, Mueller and others speak of curing Syphilis in a couple of weeks. The fact is, and I cannot impress it too strongly, no internal treatment will avail anything in the cure of chancre proper until the poisoning becomes general. Suffice it to say that Mercury, in some of its forms, will almost always answer for the cure of Syphilis proper, in an otherwise uncontaminated system.

But, unluckily a majority of the cases falling into our hands have been *poisoned with Mercury* given in huge quantities, and thus have established a disease *sui generis* or formed some difficult combination. Even Hartmann advises the saturating of the system with this crude drug in cases of phagedaenic sloughing, to the extent of intense mercurialism, very gravely informing us that even this condition is preferable to permitting the ravages of the disease. Reliable as this author usually is, and aside from the fact that we have several other remedies of equal value, in cases of phagedaena, it is very questionable which of the two poisons should be preferred.

Nitric Acid and *Iodide of Potash* are the principal remedies to be given in these cases of what may be termed Mercurio-Syphilitic poisoning, the former being more particularly indicated when the glands and mucous surfaces are involved, and the latter when there is rapid degeneration of the tissue, sloughing and a tendency to gangrene. It is also a remedy of great importance in ptyalism and salivation, as also in those eruptive conditions where there is a tendency to serous rather than mucous secretion. In cases of sloughing characterized by great prostration we should give *Arsenicum* or *Iodide of Arsenic;* but if the sloughing be accompanied by unusually severe symptoms of cachexia, *Lachesis* or *Crotalus* will best subserve our purpose.

For the skin affections, when not the result of Mercury, this remedy may be given, particularly for those in which there is a tendency to the formation of pus. In the different forms of Erythema Eczema or Exanthema, *Cantharis* should receive our first consideration and next in prominence should be ranked *Apis.* and *Lycopodium.* In eruptions of a phlyzacious appearance, perhaps *Lachesis* claims the first thought. For the various manifestations of Squama, *Arsenicum, Hep. Sulph., Graphite* or *Calcarea.*

For diseases of the bones, if from Mercury, give *Aurum, Mezereum,* the *Iodide* or *Hydriodate* of *Potassa* or *Silicia.* If from a mercurio-scrofulous cause, there may be added *Hep. Sulph., Calc.* and *Stillingia.* For Allopecia, *Nat. Mur., Nitric or Muriatic Acid.*

Thuja., internally, cures most forms of condyloma, and internally and externally, with the addition of *Nitric Acid* and the knife, has never failed me in Sycotic excrescences of whatever shape.

Other remedies suggest themselves for the almost innumerable accompaniments of *Lues*, but the most important for all practical purposes, have been enumerated; in fact I have had no occasion to use any other. Nor has it been thought proper to give anything more than the leading indications for their use. The *particular* symptoms calling for the administration of the remedy will prove a profitable study.

To sum up: True Syphilis, alone, is not the terrible disease, in itself—although bad enough—which we have been taught to believe. Its secondary stage can always be prevented by local treatment of the primary chancre, if speedily discovered. It is contagious, but not now infectious. It is inoculable only, as I believe, through its pus. It never affects osseous structures, except indirectly. It is not hereditary; and I go farther, and even question the hereditary nature of any disease other than scrofula. Sycosis has no necessary connection with syphilis; if developing only itself, it is easy of cure, but is frequently complicated, a consequence of its so often being found in bad company. Finally, Syphilis yields much more readily to homœopathic, than any other form of medication; but we should bear in mind the fact that to be successful, we should generally employ the low attenuations.

I beg to close this paper with a report of a remarkable cure of a surgical case by the administration of medicine—a cure which was effected altogether unexpectedly and accidentally. My friend Mr. Witte of Cleveland, the well-known Pharmaceutist, kindly transcribed the case from the records of the U. S. Marine Hospital, while under my charge.

Mr. ——, of brig Ellen White, age 32, nativity Ireland, was admitted to hospital Aug. 14, 1869. The cause of admission was *dysentery*, but investigation revealed the fact that he had for a long time been, and was then, suffering from Syphilitic dyscrasia. There were also three complete fistulous openings into the rectum, but whether connected with syphilitic origin I was never able to satisfactorily determine. At the date of first examination he was suffering from tenesmus, bloody and mucous stools, averaging one every half hour and accompanied with a general febrile condition. He was immediately ordered *Merc. Sol.* 2d c. trit. every two hours, with the effect of relieving the dysenteric character of the discharges; but on the third day the stools assumed a watery, sanious appearance; there was frequent thirst, great prostration, &c., for which, on the 16th in the evening *Ars. Alb.* 3d c. was prescribed, a dose every two hours. This was continued until the 17th, when purely dysenteric symptoms re-appeared, but the evacuations were pure mucous and attended with little pain. At this time *Petroleum* 5th c. was given. Thence up to the 5th of October, he alternated between a watery diarrhœa and mucous discharges, every four or five days. *Merc.*, *Arsenicum*, *Petroleum*, *China* and *Carb. Veg.* were successively given. At this time an abscess made its appearance upon inner side of right thigh, increasing in volume until the 11th, when deep-seated fluctuation was detected, and on the 14th it was opened, giving vent to a discharge of bloody, offensive and purulent matter which continued to exude in large quantity, gradually becoming serous and sanious and without prospect of granulation, until the 31st when an injection of Nitrate of Silver, 10 grains to the ounce of water, was ordered. This was repeated every other day, some four or five times, together with the administration of *Hep. Sulph.* 5th c. followed by *Calc. Carb.* 5th c. trit., which were continued until Dec. 1, when the patient was discharged *cured*. Now, what is remarkable about the case is this: Two months previous to his discharge, I had thoroughly explored the fistulas with a view to an operation, but from the nature of the case had waited for a favorable opportunity. Without occupying your time with a statement of the first appearance and general improvement of the fistulas, I will simply say that they were thoroughly healed, *without any local interference*, at the date of the patient's discharge; and although he remained with me for several months thereafter in the capacity of Janitor, there was no indication of the recurrence of either of the original conditions, under which he was admitted to the ward. The case is one of so extraordinary a nature that I have added it to this already long paper, even at the risk of exhausting your patience.

A word more, and I am done. Many years since my father, Prof. A. O. Blair, called my attention to the appropriate use of *animal poisons* in all cases of blood poisoning, that is, those of a *generic* nature. Repeated observation has convinced me that here is a "lead" which, if properly followed will result in the development of a clue to the treatment of this class of diseases, hitherto unthought of. Instance the use of *Lachesis, Cantharis, Apis,* &c., in Syphilis, Erysipelas and Scarlatina, respectively, and you may possibly evolve a train of thought and experimentation which will result in untold benefit to future generations.

Incidentally my attention was last evening called to a very important omission in this paper, viz: the mention of *Iritis*. Briefly, then, this disease may always be considered one of Syphilitic or Scrofulous origin and I think it safe to say that nine times in ten it is the result of the former. To be accurate, as far as my own experience goes, I have never seen a case in which the Syphilitic poisoning could not be traced. You who are familiar with a true Iritis will readily call to mind its peculiar appearance — will remember particularly the fixed appearance of the pupil as it is drawn inward and upward, the papular tubercles of iris and the peculiar reddish-brown appearance they assume. Further on they ulcerate, the various coats as well as the muscular tissues become involved and utter destruction of the eye is imminent. *Aconite, Belladonna* and *Atropia,* so often urged, may suit an early stage of the disease when simple inflammation, perhaps contraction and dilatation of the pupil, are the only premonitory indications visible; but when a certain knowledge of its Syphilitic nature is developed, we must resort to *Iodide of Mercury, Lachesis, Crotalus, Iodide of Potash, Graphites or Silicea.*

Report on Improved Methods of Treating Various Surgical Diseases.

BY PROF. DANFORTH, OF HAHNEMANN MEDICAL COLLEGE, CHICAGO.

There is little new (that I know to be useful) to report in the department of Medicine in Surgical Practice. And yet, our faith in the old remedies has been fully sustained, and, I may say, greatly strengthened. Lachesis and Arsenicum, in gangrene, have both proved of indispensible value; Aconite, Arnica, Bell., Hamamelis and Rhus. Tox., have proved themselves invaluable again and again. Quite a number of cases of venereal warts and condyloma have been speedily cured by the use of Thuya., 200 c.; also by Nit. Acid, 200 c.

In the department of *Operative Surgery*, some new and useful information seems to have been gathered. At the Hahnemann Hospital, in our city, the surgical department of which is under my charge, several operations have been made which, if not entirely new, may yet deserve mention, by way of illustrating what we are doing on the Lake Shore.

The first was on an Ovarian Tumor, operated on before the College Class last October by galvano puncture. The tumor was of one year's growth, in a lady 29 years of age, *married*, though not living with husband; tumor distinct, well defined — as large as a child's head – in right side, attended with a good deal of pain and general debility. Patient under Ether; three gold needles ($3\frac{1}{2}$ in. long) passed through abdominal walls into tumor, whole length; attached a 24 cell zinc and carbon battery charged with Bi Chromate Potass., Sulphuric Acid and water; negative pole to needles, positive (sponge) electrode to left thigh; continued current 25 minutes. Patient experienced a great deal of abdominal pain for ten hours after the operation — vomiting also — finally quieting down under the use of Aconite and Bell., 30 c. She remained one week at the Hospital, and left for home (five miles distant) in good spirits, with no sign of the tumor present. Immediately after the removal of the needles the fluid contents of the tumor ran out into the abdomen and I feared that we had only accomplished an evacuation of the sack, or cyst, and that it would refill within a month or two, but I have reliable information from the lady, five months after the operation, to the effect that she still remains well, with no appearance of a return of the tumor.

This operation is not new, and yet I believe this case is one of the best pronounced and most satisfactory results yet obtained from the use of the galvanic current. Unfortunately, we cannot expect to cure all cases of Ovarian Tumor with galvanism, it is only recent cases of *fluid cysts* that come within reach of the needle treatment, (not that it is necessary to evacuate the cyst,) but it is necessary that the needle should be brought into contact with fluid in order to produce "Electrolysis" (i e., the decomposition of compound substances,) before the tumor can be discussed; hence, galvanism is of *very little practical value* in the treatment of solid tumors, but, upon the contrary, of great, I may say indispensable, value in the treatment of vascular and cystic growths.

"Excision of head of femur for Hip Disease." Morbus Coxarius is a long-continued and very troublesome disease, most frequently terminating fatally.

A boy nine years of age, suffering from this disease for two years, was brought to our hospital for treatment last November. The left hip was alone involved; leg flexed, and fixed at hip, as though anchylosis had taken place. On the outer part of the limb, just below the greater trochanter was a sinus discharging pus. The probe, introduced through this sinus, falls upon rough bone, though it requires considerable probing to elicit roughness. The question of an operation in such a case as this is one that is likely to cause the surgeon a great deal of solicitude.

I believe it is now well established, however, that excision ought *not* to be practiced before *pus forms*, and, as a rule, ought to be *thereafter*. In this case, however, we have anchylosis fixing the limb in a very awkward position, and we can only feel a roughness of bone on most *thorough probing*, leaving us still in doubt about the propriety of operating.

However, an incision was made in the line of the femur just posterior to the trochanter major and dissection carried down to the head of the femur, when we found both the head and neck completely carious. The head was lifted from the acetabulum, the chain saw passed around just below the trochanter major, and the bone severed. The acetabulum was not affected, though a cartilaginous formation about the head of femur had fixed it in anchylosis. The wound was cleansed and closed with interrupted silver sutures. Boy re-acted well. A good deal of suppuration followed for two weeks, wound being cleansed often with Calendula and Carbolic Acid. The boy was confined to bed with extension of limb by weight and pulley for thirty days, *finally* recovering with a useful limb; can walk on it readily, though it is some two inches shorter than its fellow.

The point I want to make in this case, is this: "Excision of the hip should always be advised, in children under ten years of age, when there is an open sinus communicating with carious bone." It is a duty we owe to our patients, and one that will richly repay for the toil and danger incident to the work.

Dr. Sayers, of New York, puts his patients into wire breeches immediately after the operation and allows them to move about daily, and claims that it is a great improvement over the extension treatment.

"Hæmorrhoids." Some improvement in their treatment has been discovered and practiced the past year that I deem important (i.e., their removal with "Dr. Knott's Rectilinear Ecraseur," which, after all, is but an improved clamp, which gives the surgeon *complete* control of his case and work). I have operated on fourteen cases—three at our Hospital and the balance in private practice—and in *every instance* the result was *entirely* satisfactory. I know of no other mode of treatment of which I could speak so favorably. The instrument is a *strong* clamp, having a slot in one blade into which a dull, knife-like projection from the other, fits, the closure of which crushes the hæmorrhoidal tumor so completely that it never troubles the patient again. Of course, I would not advise the removal of every hœmorrhoidal tumor met with, but I would advise the use of Knott's Clamp in the treatment of every case where an operation was deemed necessary. It is far superior to the ligature, removing, as it does (if used thoroughly) every vestige of the diseased growth, and, as a rule, leaving the patient *free* from pain within ten hours after the operation

Surgical Cases.

REPORTED BY DR. DICKINSON, OF DES MOINES.

Two cases of oblique fracture of femur in middle third. Patients ten and twelve years of age. Treated by applying three short splints to thigh and extension bar with perineal band. Produced extension at foot with strips of adhesive plaster along sides of the leg carried through a tourniquet screw, in absence of other apparatus.

Excellent recovery in one case; in the other, no shortening, but curvature of the bone forward. The parents in this last case undertook the care of the patient themselves, after the second week, in spite of my protest to the contrary.

A fatty tumor in internal superior angle of the orbit of the left eye. Operated on by slitting open the conjunctiva and dissecting out.

Schirrhous tumor on lower lip, near angle. Took out V-shaped portion of lip and closed wound with silver needles and figure of 8 suture.

A child one-and-a-half years old fell, violently striking the chin on the floor; the tongue was caught between the teeth and bitten completely in two for more than half its width, and two-thirds of an inch from the point. Nothing was done for a week, when the child was brought for treatment. The wound had not united, and the edges had nearly healed.

The edges of the wound were pared and brought together with an interrupted suture of fine silk. The wound healed kindly, and an unpleasant disfigurement was obviated.

With the exception of the fractures, all these cases were operated on in conjunction with Dr. Carter of this city.

BUREAU OF OBSTETRICS.

P. H. WORLEY, M. D., Des Moines, Chairman.

PUERPERAL CONVULSIONS, by GEO. H. BLAIR, M. D.

I wish to consider, very briefly, the subject of Puerperal Convulsions. I do this for a double purpose: First, To give expression to my own conscientious views; and, second, To invite the criticism of this learned body.

To the novice in medicine — to him who has yet to battle with the rarer and deadlier diseases of human life — but a faint conception of the horrible nature of this affection can be entertained. Even to the old and experienced practitioner, the term Eclampsia calls up recollections sufficient to cause a shudder. The delicate circumstances under which the disease occurs — the suddenness of the attack and the necessity for prompt and efficient treatment — the awful suffering and contortions of the patient — the terrible anxiety and disposition for interference by the relatives and friends; and, above all, the responsibility which attaches to the safety or loss of perhaps two lives, renders the subject of this essay of the gravest importance.

And first, let me not be misunderstood. Puerperal Convulsions, in the true sense, is an exceeding rare disease; and should not be confounded — as it frequently, and very conveniently for the reputation of the practitioner, is — with Epilepsy, Chorea, and more often with Hysteria. Apoplexy, which frequently is, in fact, an incident of the disease, and Epilepsy also, may sometimes so closely simulate it upon a cursory examination, as to confuse and mislead the most acute observer; but, since the first is in reality very often a concomitant of the disease, and amenable to the same treatment; and, since the character of the latter will soon reveal itself, we need not long suffer by an error of diagnosis. There is no apology, however, for confounding it with hysteria in any form.

Let me, for the purpose of greater completeness, hastily sketch its character as it naturally presents itself, and briefly also, hint at the differential aspect of the disease as compared with those with which it is most liable to be confused.

Puerperal Convulsions are most apt to occur in the *primipara*, yet they may take place in subsequent pregnancies, more rarely. They are most frequently met with between the seventh and ninth month, yet instances are recorded of their existence in all stages of child-bearing life. They usually occur during, or are accompanied by, labor, although this is not necessarily the case. [Case: Fourteen hours after delivery.]

The first prominent indication of the disease, is the sudden supervention of head ache of an exceedingly violent character, usually occupying a circumscribed space. The appearance of this symptom during pregnancy, independent of any other well-defined cause, should always excite our most serious apprehensions. The intensity of the pain rapidly increases, accompanied by obscurity of vision, and indistinctness of speech; and convulsions speedily follow. The legs and arms are violently convulsed; the face is horribly distorted; the eyes rolled up; the tongue protrudes; saliva issues from the mouth — indeed, the general appearance is much that of Epilepsy. After the lapse of a few minutes the paroxysm gradually subsides and the patient sinks into a state of perfect coma. The breathing now becomes labored and stertorous; the face is blue, puffed and turgid — in short, presents all the indications of Apoplexy. This condition may last for a half hour or more, when the patient begins to moan, becomes restless and tosses about; delirium manifests itself, sometimes even resulting in a furious mania, to be followed by a repetition of the convulsions and coma.

It differs from Epilepsy in the absence of the characteristic scream which precedes the latter; by the entire absence of consciousness after the coma disappears, and in the character of the circulation — in advanced stages of Puerperal Convulsions the pulse being imperceptible at the extremities.

It would hardly be proper in a body of medical men to discuss the distinctions between this disease and the various forms of eccentric convulsions — those due to reflex nervous action excited by indigestion, morbid secretions in the intestines, and, more frequently, from uterine irritation, that almost universal cause, remote or direct, of hysteria, in all its various phases. Nor would this subject have been alluded to were it not that I am well convinced that cases of this nature have been confounded with true Puerperal Convulsions; and because, in advocating a certain mode of treatment I wish the real nature of the disease to be taken into consideration.

Let me be understood, therefore, as speaking of *Centric Convulsions* — those due to pressure upon the spinal cord from an increased volume of blood and congestion of the capillaries.

The *cause* of this disease is supposed to be due, in many instances, to toxæmic influences, and the almost universal presence of albuminaria gives strength to this view; it may be occasioned by excessive mental excitement, by indigestion, &c.; but these should rather be looked upon as *auxiliaries*, than as prime causes. In my judgment, the commonest, as well as the most natural causes may be found in the pressure of the gravid womb upon the lower branches of the Aorta, cutting off a free circulation in the lower extremities, as is so frequently evidenced by the œdema of these parts in the pregnant female—thus occasioning a super-abundance of blood in the brain and upper portion of the body. The fact of the disease occurring most often in the *primipara*, when the pressure is necessarily greater than in subsequent pregnancies—the fact of its generally coming on during the latter months, when the period of pressure is greatest—the fact that recovery is not deemed possible until the removal of the fœtus—all these go to substantiate the theory.

I shall not undertake to speak, at this time, of those rare cases of con-vulsions occurring in anemia, where the blood-vessels, instead of being found engorged are entirely emptied of their contents. No cases of this character have come under my observation, and hence, in speaking of treatment, they are not to be considered.

As before remarked, the disease is exceedingly rare, but one case occurring in six or seven hundred labors. In my own experience, extending over twenty-two years, ten cases have come under my own direct charge, and I have seen, in consultation, nearly as many more. While the mortality under what is called "Old School" treatment averages one in four, or twenty-five per cent., and while, under what is termed Homœopathic treatment, I am convinced the mortality is even still greater, I may be permitted in justification of the course I have pursued—and not because any personal merit is involved—to state, that of the ten cases of my own, there occurred but one death—and in this case a *post mortem* revealed rupture and extravasation; and in those cases where I had the honor to be consulted, where the views of the attending physician coincided with my own, the result was alike satisfactory.

Our Homœopathic therapeutics—the treatment prescribed in our books—has proved to me, highly unsatisfactory. Aside from the unfortunate results following, I think it susceptible of demonstration that the law of "Similia" is here entirely inapplicable and should be ignored. Early indoctrinated in the Hahnemannian faith—a faith from which, I thank God, I have never departed—I confess that our records in Eclampsia have been to me a disappointment and a mortification. But more matured thought and a riper judgment have convinced me that in the treatment of this disease we should discard the considerations which are applied to morbid affections in general, and view it from an independent stand-point.

Pertinent to this position, let us inquire into the pathological conditions present in this disease. [And here, by the way, we must recognize the importance of this much neglected—by our school—branch of science.] We find an intensely congested state of the capillaries of the brain, frequently to such an extent as to deprive the vessels of their circulation entirely and attended by effusion into the surrounding cavities. A state of utter stagnation is imminent. Under such circumstances no system of mere medication is available. We should discard all thoughts of creeds or doctrinal points, or "pathies," and view the case with a surgical or mechanical eye, so to speak. If we find an individual suffocating from the pressure of a rope, common sense dictates its removal, before using other means for restoration. If a foreign substance is imbedded in the muscles, it must first be abstracted before secondary measures of relief are to be applied. And so, gentlemen, should we view the case under consideration. The force of the circulation must be speedily lessened. The intense engorgement of the blood-vessels of the brain must be relieved, and we should aim to induce speedy dilitation of the the *os uteri* in order to promptly and safely deliver. To accomplish these results we have a remedy in the *Lancet*. Its use under such circumstances does not in the least conflict with our faith in the law of *Similia*. The state of the case is such, indeed, as to have no relation to theories of simply medicinal cure. There are those among our Old School brethren who denounce this mode of treatment, as well as in our own. But I apprehend the objection arises in a great measure from the ill-success attending this method in years gone by. Venesection in olden times was quite a different thing from what it now is. Until within a comparatively modern period, to abstract beyond ten or fifteen ounces of blood was considered a very dangerous proceeding. Indeed, the first suggestion of the propriety of taking large quantities was induced by the gratifying results which followed upon an accidental hemorrhage from a misplaced bandage. Hence, the older writers looked upon Puerperal Convulsions as almost necessarily fatal. If the practitioner saved one-half his patients he was deemed particularly fortunate. The decreased mortality following the adoption of free venesection is of itself sufficient evidence in its favor. But let it be firmly impressed that the amount of blood drawn should not be sparing. Instead of ten ounces, take forty, or fifty, or sixty — and do it boldly and without hesitation, if you would attain a beneficial result.

I have spoken of the lancet as the remedy of paramount importance, but we should not neglect auxiliary measures. In case the fœtus is still *in utero* our object will be to remove it as soon as possible, and for this purpose I need not remind you, gentlemen, of the importance of version, of instrumental aid, &c. Nor need I recapitulate the medicinal remedies, which, in connection with the lancet, are of so much value — nay more, are of sufficient importance in themselves, in some instances, to effect a cure. My object has not been to write an exhaustive treatise, but simply to give you the well-considered result of observation and experience. One or two suggestions arise, however, to which I would call your attention.

You are all aware of the almost universal recommendation of ice and ice-cold water to the head in the disease under consideration. I wish I could impress you with the barbarity of this treatment. By this means you are conducing directly to the object it is your aim to obviate — you are adding to the cause of congestion, rather than preventing. If water be used at all, — and it is of minor importance, — let it be applied *warm* in this, as in *all other* congestions or inflammations.

I wish to call your attention, too, to the use of Caulophyllin in aiding the woman in avoiding the perils of child-birth. In my own hands, and those of other practitioners of my acquaintance, its effects have been marvelous.

In connection with the subject of Eclampsia, I wish to correct an important error — at least it seems one to me — the very general belief that persons of short, stout build and full habits are peculiarly liable to this disease and apoplexy; that is, that peculiar conformation contributes to an attack. My own observation does not justify this conclusion; and I may add that an expression of the observation and experience of the members of the Cuyahoga Co. Med. Association bears me out in the opinion that the disease is more apt to depend upon mental than physical organization.

Puerperal Convulsions, with Instrumental Delivery.

BY A. O. HUNTER, M. D., OF DES MOINES, IOWA.

I was called on the morning of the twentieth of February to a Mrs. W., aged twenty, of billious-lymphatic temperament, closely built, of strong muscular fibre, broad shoulders, and short, thick neck, who had had premonitory symptoms of labor for several hours previous. (Primipara.)

On making an examination I found the os uteri dilating nicely, without any peculiarity whatever observable.

The pelvis was large and well formed. Head presenting — not large. She continued having pains regularly, and was cheerful and pleasant throughout the day, the os dilating slowly.

About seven p. m., os seemed dilated to the size of a half-dollar or perhaps a little larger. Eight p. m., she complained of dizziness, blindness, &c.

Bathed her head in cold water, and gave her a few drops of Gelseminum, but in a few moments she was in a convulsion.

She was delivered in a few minutes after the second paroxsym with the aid of the forceps and, after removing with difficulty a firmly adhering placenta, she was placed in a comfortable position, where she remained unconscious — in deep coma — with stertorous breathing for five or six hours. When consciousness returned, she had no recollection of the delivery of the child or of the placenta.

One peculiar feature in her case, was that every evening about eight o'clock she would be threatened with convulsions, and it seemed almost impossible to prevent their return, for three successive evenings, when the symptoms gradually grew lighter each day. After the fourteenth day no more symptoms appeared. Treatment: Gels. 1st., ten drops in half tumbler of water, two teaspoonfuls every hour through the day.

Bathing the head in cold water and the feet in warm water seemed to give relief just before the paroxysm.

This is the only case of recovery of Puerperal Convulsions in our city this spring. I believe six cases are reported all of which died under Allopathic treatment.

Case of Extra Uterine Pregnancy.

REPORTED BY W. H. DICKINSON, M. D., OF DES MOINES.

In the summer of 1872 Mrs. B., of Atlantic, Iowa, became, as she supposed enciente. Gestation proceeded favorably for the first five months, when symptoms of abortion appeared, which were speedily controlled by the attending physician.

When her full time had elapsed, according to her calculation, slight labor pains set in and her physician was summoned to her assistance. An examination showed that the os was not at all dilated, neither was it dilatable; neither could the position of the child's head or trunk be detected. The physician was puzzled by this anomalous condition of things, but, as the pains soon after subsided, he concluded to wait for further developments, supposing that it might be a case of false labor.

But, in a few days abnormal symptoms developed themselves.

The abdomen became tympanitic and respiration difficult, the patient unable to lie down, but compelled to remain propped up on the bed or reclining in a chair; the complexion sallow; some pain in right groin and hypochondrium and an occasional escape of fetid gas from the uterus.

A council of physicians was called. Examination showed no dilatation of the os and no well marked presentation. The tumor seemed to be on the right of median line, and some doubt was expressed as to whether it was not tumor of the right ovary.

An effort was made to dilate the os with the finger, but it seemed quite rigid and resisted the introduction of either the finger or sound.

In a few days the patient died and a post mortem examination revealed a case of tubal pregnancy, the fetus being well developed.

I regret that I could not get a detailed account of the case from the physician in charge, and am only able to give meagre outlines of it. I saw the patient, during a visit to Atlantic, about a week before her death, but failed to make a correct diagnosis.

BUREAU OF CLINICAL MEDICINE.

C. PEARSON, M. D., of Mt. Pleasant, Chairman.

FISTULA IN ANO, by A. O. HUNTER, M. D., of Des Moines.

Mrs. D., aged forty-two, a large, fleshy woman, had a very severe attack of bilious fever during the fall of 1872, suffering most of the time with gastric derangement, nausea, vomiting, with some diarrhea.

During days of convalescence a large abscess formed in the ischio-rectal fossa which was very painful and gave her a great deal of trouble in defacation. Was poulticed, lanced, and discharged freely, but did not heal; kept on discharging for several weeks, the feces streaked with pus tinged slightly with blood.

On making an examination from the opening, which was large enough to admit the point of the little finger, and about an inch from the anus, a probe passed readily through it into the bowel and was felt about three-quarters of an inch from the margin of the anus by the finger, which had been previously introduced.

Her general health was good now, and the case appeared to be one that might be healed without incision; but, as she was most desirous to be cured as quickly as possible, I determined to divide the parts, which I did on the following day, and in about four weeks she was entirely well.

A Case Illustrating the Effects of Water as a Remedial Agent.

BY P. J. CONNELLY, M. D., OF DES MOINES.

A young man about twenty years of age came to my office to consult me about a sore leg which had been troubling him for ten years. He gave me its history as follows:

In playing with another boy he received a kick on the shin, about mid-way between the ankle and knee. It became inflamed, badly swollen for a month, suppurated and discharged freely a yellowish matter for one year. In one month after this discharge commenced necrosis supervened, and in a short time seventeen pieces of bone were thrown off with the discharge of matter — the pieces varying from half to three-fourths of an inch in length. At the end of the year the discharge ceased. Since that time the young man has suffered constantly with a sore, aching pain, which had made gradual advance until the thigh became implicated. There were but short remissions of the pain at times, always followed by exacerbation when at rest. Thus have eight years of his life been spent in pain and suffering. After hearing his story, on examination I found his leg cold, (he said it had been so for some time previous,) atrophied so that the circumference of the thigh was two inches less than the other, unable to bear any weight on it, and constantly aching.

Treatment: I gave him a few drops of Silicea and Rhus. Tox, to be taken at long intervals, from which I expected no result, and in which I was not disappointed, nor did I, in fact, expect to give him any relief, for he had been treated and mistreated a great deal during the time.

I now ordered him to keep quiet for a week or two; to take a large coffee pot, fill it with cold water, strip himself so that another person could pour its contents gradually over the whole length of his leg from the hip down to the toes three times a day, at the height of two feet from the limb, and if through the night his pains should trouble him, get up and repeat the application, rub well with a coarse towel; continue for a week and then report. This he did, and at the end of a week his report was as unexpected as it was gratifying — the pains were decidedly less severe, could use it better, and slept more. Continued the treatment. After another week, reported a more decided improvement. After two months he reports no pain, can follow his plow all day, rests well at night, circulation established, the muscles regaining their tonicity, the young man getting well, and to cold water belongs the glory.

Addison's Disease.

BY DR. T. A. BENBOW, NEW PROVIDENCE, IOWA.

I must acknowledge that I have never seen a well-written treatise upon this very rare, and generally fatal, disease. I do not wonder that the busy practitioner often finds it difficult, when called upon, to treat this disease with any degree of success, to the comfort of relatives and friends; and those of us who have had any experience in the treatment of this disease, surely owe to the profession our experience.

I now give in brief, the symptoms and treatment of a case treated by me last winter and spring. Was called Feb. 15th; found the patient — a man aged 57 — in the following condition: Some febrile excitement, pulse one hundred; a beating and throbbing in the region of the left kidney, extending around in the left loin, with a bruised pain in the same region, worse from contact; a drawing downwards in the whole of the left side; slight pain in the region of the stomach, with occasional vomiting of a slimy, mucous substance; anemia and great feebleness of the heart's action. When he wished to lie down, he would first get upon his knees and elbows and remain in that position for some minutes, then gradually lower himself down upon either side, when he could remain tolerably comfortable so long as he was quiet, but just turning over in bed, or turning around upon a chair would increase the frequency of the pulse from ten to fifteen beats per minute; hot flashes over that portion of his body upon which he would be lying; a constant rattling cough, with a viscid, stringy expectoration, of a bluish color, no doubt from the "elimination of the excrementitious renal accumulations in the blood; the cellular structure becoming engorged, and effusions occurring more or less extensive." The patient, much of the time, was very much indisposed to either bodily or mental exertion; great loss of memory; appetite variable—sometimes a little, but most of the time none at all; eyes glassy and pearly; the body very much wasted, but no dryness or shrivelled appearance of the skin; general enlargement of the lymphatic glands all over the body. The characteristic discoloration of the skin was perhaps not as marked as if both kidneys had been affected, but there was that peculiar dingy, smoky, bronze color upon the forehead, face, neck and hands; not so much upon other portions of the body.

The patient had been feeling quite dull and indisposed for four months previous to my call; had been treated for two months by one of the *Regulars* for "Liver Complaint and Lung Disease," but had been without medicine for one month when I first saw him, so that there was a clear case, without any drug symptoms.

Treatment: Aconite 2x, Nux 3x, given alternately one hour apart.

Feb. 16th. Pulse 85; much of the throbbing and bruised feeling gone; the vomiting and distress about the stomach no better. Continued the treatment.

Feb. 17th. A very little more strength; the hot flashes nearly all gone; vomiting some better.

Feb. 18th. Some improvement in every respect except his cough; this distressed and alarmed him more than all else.

Feb. 22d. Almost at a stand-still, except that his cough grew worse. I now gave him Kali-bichrom 2x, and Arsenicum 12 c., to be given two hours apart alternately.

Feb. 23d. Some little improvement in every respect except his cough, which was a little worse. He now became very anxious that I should do something for his cough, but I soon gave him to understand that his lungs were not at fault, and that at the proper time he would perhaps get better of his cough.

Feb. 26th. Better in every respect; has not coughed nearly so much for two days. Continued the same medicines at much longer intervals.

March 4th. Has not coughed any for two days and nights; feels much stronger; can sit up some of the time in a chair. Continued the medicines—one dose per day of each.

March 20th. Pulse soft, easily compressed, but he feels much stronger; more appetite; can walk about the room. I now gave the medicines on alternate days.

April 1st. Is now able to go out and walk about the farm; still feels quite feeble. I now discontinued all medicine.

April 14. Is now able to do some light work, but not feeling entirely well; the discoloration of the face and hands is still to be seen to some extent; the enlargement of the glands has nearly all disappeared.

CONSTITUTION AND BY-LAWS

OF THE SOCIETY OF

HOMŒOPATHIC PHYSICIANS

OF IOWA.

—•→

ADOPTED MAY 31, 1870.

—

CONSTITUTION.

ARTICLE I.

This Society shall be known as the "SOCIETY OF HOMŒOPATHIC PHYSICIANS OF IOWA," having for an object the advancement of Medical Science, and the dissemination of the law of "*Similia Similibus Curantur.*"

ARTICLE II.

The officers of the Society shall consist of a President, two Vice-Presidents, a Secretary and Treasurer. At each annual meeting an election, by ballot, shall be held for the above named officers.

There shall also be elected by the society, in the above manner, at each annual meeting, a Board of Censors, consisting of five members, a majority of whom shall constitute a quorum for the transaction of business.

A majority of the members present shall be necessary for the election of any of the above named officers, and they shall hold their offices for the term of one year, or until others shall have been elected to fill their places.

ARTICLE III.

The duties of the respective officers shall be such as may from time to time be prescribed by the By-Laws.

ARTICLE IV.

The Society shall hold at least one session in each year, at such time and place as the majority of the members present at the last annual meeting may determine.

ARTICLE V.

At any meeting of the Society, five members shall constitute a quorum

ARTICLE VI.

No physician who is not a graduate, and who has commenced the practice of Homœopathy since 1870, shall be admitted as a member of this Society.

ARTICLE VII.

This Constitution may be altered or amended by a two-third vote of the members attending; provided, however, that at the meeting previous, notice has been given in writing of such alteration or amendment.

— ⬩◆⬩ —

BY-LAWS.

DUTIES OF THE PRESIDENT.

SECTION 1. The President shall preside at all the meetings of the Society, preserve order therein, put all questions, announce the decisions, and appoint the committees not otherwise ordered; direct the Secretary to call extraordinary meetings upon the written request of members, not less than six in number, giving reasons for such action.

DUTIES OF THE VICE-PRESIDENTS.

SECTION 2. The Vice-Presidents shall perform, in the order of their election, in the absence of the President, all duties appertaining to the office of President.

DUTIES OF THE SECRETARY.

SECTION 3. The Secretary shall provide a suitable book for records, and note therein all the resolutions and proceedings of the Society; note the names of members and the date of their admission. It shall be his duty to file the annual reports of Bureaus and Committees, and any other matter as ordered by the Society. He shall answer all letters addressed to the Society, open and maintain such correspondence as may advance its interests; give notice, at least two weeks before hand, of the meetings of the Society; notify candidates of their election, and the members of the several Bureaus and Committees of their appointment, stating the subjects assigned to them.

DUTIES OF TREASURER.

SECTION 4. The Treasurer shall collect all moneys belonging to the Society, make the necessary disbursements, and report annually in writing to the Censors.

DUTIES OF CENSORS.

SECTION 5. The Censors shall carefully and impartially examine into the qualifications of each candidate for membership, in accordance with the standard of qualification laid down by a majority of the Society; shall examine the report of the Treasurer and report the same to the Society, and shall state, after the name of each applicant for membership, the College and Class in which such applicant graduated.

MEMBERS.

SECTION 6. The Society may elect members permanently, according to the standard adopted.

Honorary members may be elected by a two-third vote, but not exceeding two at each annual meeting. Persons so elected shall be entitled to all the privileges of membership except the right of voting.

FEES.

SECTION 7. An initiation fee of $3.00 shall be paid by each newly elected member, and in addition thereto an annual fee of $2.00 at each subsequent meeting. A failure to pay, after one year, shall subject such delinquent to suspension until such time as his arrearages are made up.

PAPERS AND COMMUNICATIONS.

SECTION 8. Any original paper or communication read before this Society shall be considered the property of the reader, of which he alone is to be responsible, but with his consent and that of the Publishing Committee, may appear in the published proceedings; or, if rejected by said Committee, shall be returned to the writer with liberty to publish in any medical journal, if so disposed.

ETHICS.

SECTION 9. The code of Ethics as adopted by the American Institute of Homœopathy shall be held to govern the members of this Society.

BUREAUS AND COMMITTEES.

SECTION 10. The following Bureaus and Committees shall be annually appointed by the President, consisting of not less than two members, to report in writing at each annual meeting:

1. *Materia Medica and Provings*—Which shall obtain facts relating to Materia Medica; and institute, collect and arrange provings of drugs.

2 *Clinical Experience*—Which shall collect facts relating to Clinical Medicine.

3. *Obstetrics and Diseases of Women and Children*—Which shall collect and report facts and observations on the subjects pertaining thereto.

4. *Surgery*—Which shall collect all improvements in Surgery and Surgical means, especially in connection with Homœopathic treatment.

5. *Medical Education*—Which shall act in connection with the Committee appointed by the American Institute of Homœopathy.

6. *Anatomy, Physiology and Hygiene*—Which shall report to the Society the advances made in these departments of Medical Science.

7. *Medical Electricity*—Which shall report the relation of this branch of science to Homœopathic treatment.

An Executive Committee, consisting of three, shall be appointed by the President for each successive meeting, which shall arrange the necessary preliminary business of the Society, examine credentials, and do such other work as may be conducive to the efficiency of the session. The Secretary shall be *ex officio* chairman; the other members, if practicable, to reside at the place where the next annual meeting is to be held.

AMENDMENTS.

SECTION 11. These By-Laws may, by a majority vote of those present at any regular meeting, be altered or amended.

RESOLUTIONS.

The following resolutions, by Dr. Pearson, were adopted, embracing the sentiments of the Society on the liquor question:

WHEREAS, Special efforts are being made, by the enactment of local laws, to restrain the sale of intoxicating liquors; and,

WHEREAS, The Medical Profession, not without cause, has been greatly censured for demanding their sale for medical purposes; therefore,

Resolved, That this Society, representing the views of a vast majority of the Homœopathic physicians of Iowa, desires to call the attention of the public, and particularly of our law-makers, to the following statement of our views in reference to this subject:

1st. That there is but one purpose for which Alcohol is indispensable in the dispensing of medicines for the sick, viz: To preserve and hold in solution the active principle of drugs.

2d. That the sale of Tonics and Bitters (so called) is a violation of the spirit of prohibition and a fraud upon the consumer, unless they be sold under their proper name of medicated or drugged liquors.

Resolved, That we recommend to Temperance organizations the propriety of at once so changing their pledges as to prohibit their members from using alcoholic liquors "as a medicine."

Resolved, That we do not ask that the sale of whisky, brandy, malt liquors, &c., be allowed, even "for medical purposes," and we recommend our fellow-citizens to insist upon the enactment of such laws as will prohibit the sale of any alcoholic liquors whatever for such purpose, except pure alcohol only.

Resolved, That we earnestly protest against being hereafter held to any greater degree of responsibily than our fellow-citizens generally for the indiscriminate use of intoxicating liquors as "medicines," and for opening, through drug stores, a door of escape for evil-doers.

The following resolution, by Dr. Benbow, was adopted:

Resolved, That Committees of different Bureaus, and all persons giving their clinical experience, are requested to give the attenuation of the medicine used, and the frequency of the dose.

On motion of Dr. Dickinson:

Resolved, That all members preparing cases on special subjects send them to Chairmen of respective Bureaus at least thirty days before the annual meeting.

On motion of Dr. Coggswell;

Resolved, That all papers presented to the Society, subject to action of the Publishing Committee, be sent to Secretary within thirty days after adjournment.

ORDER OF BUSINESS.

1. Address by the President.
2. Election of Secretary.
3. Report of Executive Committee.
4. Reading of Minutes of previous meeting.
5. Election of Permanent and Honorary Members.
6. Report of Treasurer.
7. Nomination and Election of New Officers.
8. Reports of Committees appointed at the previous meeting.
9. Motions, resolutions, etc.
10. Miscellaneous Business.
11. Inauguration of New Officers.
12. Appointments of New Committees by the President.
13. Motions, resolutions, etc.
14. Reading of Reports, Communications and Essays.
15. Miscellaneous Business.
16. Unfinished Business.
17. Adjournment.

MEMBERS.

—

The figures at the left show date of membership.   The following motion was carried, May, 1871:

Moved, That those members of the Society who do not pay their due upon notification of the Secretary, be dropped from the roll of membership

See, also, Section 7 of By Laws.

1870 AUSTIN, P. A., M. D., ...Muscatine.
1872—ADAMS, NELSON, M. D., ...Iowa City.
1870 - BREWER, E., M. D ....Independence
1870—BAKER, R. F., M. D., ...Davenport.
1872—BURTON, H. B., M. D., ...Iowa City.
1875—BLAIR, G. H., M. D., ...Fairfield.
1872—BENBOW, DR. T. A .... New Providence
1870 - COGSWELL, C. H., M. D., ...Clinton.
1870 CONNELLY, P. J., M. D., ...Des Moines.
1872—CUNNINGHAM, J. W., M. D ....Council Bluffs.
1870—DICKINSON, W. H., M. D., ...Des Moines.
1871—DAYM, P, M. D., ...Dubuque.
1870—DE PUY, N. J., M. D ....Iowa Falls.
1872—DAVIS, J. W., M. D., ...Lansing.
1871 - EHINGER, G. E., M. D., ...Keokuk.
1871 *GOLDECKE, L., M. D ....Belle Plaine.
1870—GRAHAM, M. M. D., ...Independence.
1870—GILBERT, E. A, M. D ....Dubuque.
1872—GILBERT, S. H., M. D., ...Dubuque.
1870—HILLIS, L., M. D., ...Winterset
1871—HILL, R. L., M. D., ...Dubuque.
1870 - HINDMAN, D. R., M. D., ...Marion.
1870 - HOLT, L. E. B., M. D., ...Marshalltown.
1870—HUNTER, A. O., M. D .... Des Moines.
1873—HARRIS, Mrs. R. H., M. D., ... Grinnell.
1870—JACKSON, E., M. D., ...Epworth.
1870—KING, E. H., M. D., ...Clinton.

*Died, November 5th, 1873.

1870—KING, J. E., M. D., ...Eldora.
1873—KUNZE, A., M. D., ...Davenport.
1870—LILLIS, W. B., M. D., ...Marion.
1870—OLNEY, S. B., M. D., ...Fort Dodge.
1870—PALMER, O. T., M. D., ...Osceola.
1872—POTTER, DR. L. D., ...Gilman.
1870—PATCHEN, G. H., M. D., ...Burlington.
1871—PITCHER, A. C., M. D., ...Mt. Pleasant.
1871—PORTER, MRS. M. W., M. D., ...Davenport.
1870—POULSON, P. W., M. D., ...Council Bluffs.
1871—PEARSON, C., M. D., ...Mt. Pleasant.
1872—RUST, DR. J. D., ...Fayette.
1870—SEIDLITZ, G. N., M. D., ...Keokuk.
1872—SQUIRES, H. D., M. D., ...McGregor.
1870—STANLEY, G., M. D., ...Cedar Rapids.
1872—SMYTHE, FRANK, M. D., ...Iowa City.
1871—VIRGIN, W. T., M. D., ...Burlington.
1871—WHITLOCK, F. W., M. D., ...Farmington.
1870—WORLEY, P. H., M. D., ...Davenport.
1872—WHITAKER, DR. E. D., ...Union.
1873—WILSON, A., M. D., ...Ames.
1873—WILLIAMS, WM. M. D., ...Chariton.
1873—WATERMAN, R. W., M. D., ...Des Moines.
1872—YEOMANS, MRS. CLARA, M. D., ...Clinton.
1871—YEOMANS, S. P., M. D., ...Clinton.

www.ingramcontent.com/pod-product-compliance
Lightning Source LLC
Chambersburg PA
CBHW021638270326
41931CB00008B/1072